I_N

Chetan Bhagat is the author of eight bestselling novels and three non-fiction books, which have sold over twelve million copies and have been translated in over twenty languages worldwide.

The New York Times has called him 'the biggest selling author in India's history'. *Time* magazine named him as one of the 100 most influential people in the world, and Fast Company USA named him as one of the 100 most creative people in business worldwide.

Many of his books have been adapted into films and were major Bollywood blockbusters. He is also a Filmfare award-winning screenplay writer.

Chetan writes columns in the *Times of India* and *Dainik Bhaskar*, which are amongst the most influential and widely read newspapers in the country. He is also one of the country's leading motivational speakers.

Chetan went to college at IIT Delhi and IIM Ahmedabad, after which he worked in investment banking for a decade before quitting his job to become a full-time writer.

INDIA POSITIVE

NEW ESSAYS AND SELECTED COLUMNS

Chetan Bhagat

Text copyright © 2019 Chetan Bhagat

Published by Westland, Seattle

www.apub.com

Amazon, the Amazon logo, and Westland are trademarks of Amazon. com, Inc., or its affiliates.

ISBN-13: 9781542044165
ISBN-10: 1542044162

Typeset by SÜRYA, New Delhi
Printed in India by Manipal Technologies Limited, Manipal

Contents

Politics, India-style

Indianomics

Young India

India Positive

So it is 2019, and here we are on the verge of another big Lok Sabha election. It's different this time, isn't it? While there's some election fever, there's none of the frenzy of 2014. The pre-election analyses, predictions and rallies are in full swing. Each political side is making its promises, of course. They are also trading barbs and attacking their opponents. And yet, it is no 2014. The rise of Modi and his promises of 'acche din', the anger of the people towards the Congress government, the first-time mass use of social media, and the fact that these were the first general elections after anti-corruption protests reached the streets, meant that Indians were heavily invested in the 2014 elections. 'We need change' seemed to be what India was trying to say. And a commoner chaiwallah like Modi had spectacularly come to power, securing a massive mandate. The people celebrated—they had done it!

After all, this was change, wasn't it? The PM changed. The ministers changed. The party ruling the country changed. People power had spoken! Time for 'acche din' now! Bye-bye corruption, and hello, new progressive India!

The excitement of the 2014 elections carried over well after the polls. The honeymoon period of the new government was pure euphoria. When the Swacch Bharat campaign was launched and Modi came to the streets with a broom, many swooned. This was change indeed, they marvelled, look how India is changing now!

Let's cut to 2019. Ask people to be as excited as they were in 2014 about the government, and they will most likely give you nothing more than a smirk. Tell them to scream for change, and they are more likely to shrug their shoulders.

Yeah, things are different, they will say. But nothing has really changed, has it?

In fact, when I travel for my motivational talks, I sometimes ask the people I meet: 'How is life radically different for you as an individual under this BJP government versus the previous Congress government? And how much of that is due to the change in government?' Often, they struggle to find genuine answers. Here's how a typical conversation goes:

Me (talking to people in a Shatabdi train compartment): So what is different now in 2019 vs 2014?

Passenger 1: There are more smartphones, cheaper data and more internet content.

Me: That is true. But the BJP had little to do with this, as it is a worldwide phenomenon and would have happened even under another government, right?

Passenger 2: There's a lot more online shopping.

Me: Same, not really particular to this government.

Passenger 3: We have new currency notes!

Me: For sure, this may not have happened without demonetisation. Have to agree on this one.

Passenger 4: We have GST.

Me: Yes, but it affects businesses more. How about you as an individual?

Passenger 4: For me, GST is merely another name for indirect taxes I used to pay earlier.

Passenger 5: We also have some more metros, better roads in a few places and new airports.

Me: Okay!

Passenger 5 (continues): Then again, these were already in the pipeline and might have continued to happen under any other government.

Me: Anyone else?

Passenger 6: There are some policies, I am told, to give LPG, bank accounts and medical insurance to a lot of poor people.

Me: But we are talking about you, the average middle to upper middle class Indian travelling on this train. Has your life changed much? Or rather, would it have been very different if we had a different government during the last five years?

Passenger 6: (thinks … shakes head)

Me: (smiles)

Passenger 7 (watching me for a while and speaking finally): Why are you asking so many questions, anyway? It's India. Nothing really changes here.

The conversation above represents a popular opinion. Yes, things are different. And yet, not a lot has changed.

Nothing really changes here

The last passenger is right at one level. 'This is India, nothing really changes around here' is something a lot of people say in our country. I don't fully subscribe to this view as I find it an overly cynical take on the state of affairs. However, maybe because I am older (and hopefully wiser), I am more patient with alternate views and see the point these people are trying to make. After all, it is true that by now we have tried various types of governments and leaders. In the last ten years alone, we have tried:

1. The Congress (and UPA) in power
2. The BJP (and NDA) in power
3. A coalition government (like the UPA II)
4. A strong and stable majority government (like the Modi government)
5. A leader with a soft and gentle image (like PM Manmohan Singh)
6. A leader with a tough image (like PM Modi)

That is a lot of different things to try, isn't it? But despite all these changes at the top, India trudges along in much the same way. 2019 is not too different from 2009. If you are a student, it is hard to get into a good school or college (we're approaching a crisis in education, but that's a separate discussion). If you are a job seeker, it is difficult to find employment. The cities are choked and traffic is a nightmare. Government offices are still slow, dusty and corrupt. Good healthcare is either unavailable or too expensive. You need contacts and/or money to get anywhere. So the rules are different for the powerful and the well-connected. For the average Indian, life is a struggle.

The situation described above is true in 2019, but was also true in 2009. So the cynical uncle in the train who says 'This is India, nothing changes around here', isn't entirely wrong.

So, one wonders: why write books like *India Positive*? If things didn't move much from 2009 to 2019, why talk about where we need to be in 2029? For chances are we will still be here, as 'nothing changes around here'.

This is where I differ from Uncle Cynic. For the statement that *nothing has changed* isn't true. Maybe what is implied, and probably more accurate in our context, is this: *not much has changed, or things haven't changed fast enough*. That's a valid criticism. And it is quite different from 'nothing changed' or the seriously depressing 'nothing will *ever* change'.

It doesn't matter

The fact is this: even though little has changed, we still learnt three irrefutable things after experimenting with various types of governments and leaders. One, India is moving along, progressing, albeit at a slow pace. Two, no matter who is in power, your life doesn't change dramatically under any regime. Hence, irrespective of the prime minister, the ruling party or their election promises, as far as you and your individual life is concerned, *it doesn't matter.*

This 'it doesn't matter' is no cousin of the cynical 'nothing ever changes' statement. It doesn't mean one shouldn't care about who is in power. Neither does it mean that no matter who comes to power, you are screwed anyway.

What it means is simply this: India is so vast and varied in so many ways that no one leader or regime change is capable of altering the life of an average individual within the relatively short time span of a term or two in power.

This doesn't mean life won't change. But the change is not dependent on whether BJP or Congress is in power, or Mr Modi or Mr Singh being the PM. Sure, smartphones and mobile data have transformed the lives of Indians in the past decade. Online shopping changed retail. Rideshare apps altered the way people moved in our cities. Change happened, but your favourite leader or party didn't have as much to do with it as you thought it would.

There are two ways to look at this. One, it can make you feel helpless. What do you do when the government at the Centre, which got there by your vote, doesn't seem to matter so much? Two, it can be liberating. It tells you something else. That by coming out on the streets in 2011 or voting for change in 2014, you have now tried it all. Now, in order to really change your life, you cannot rely on politics or a particular leader. The solution is going to be someone else. The solution is going to be *you*!

Being India Positive

If 2009 was the UPA/coalition government/soft PM experiment, and 2014 was the NDA/majority government/tough PM experiment, maybe it is time in 2019 to do something different. Rather than relentlessly trying to get the perfect government in place, maybe we can try to work on ourselves. For instance, rather than counting on the government to give us jobs, maybe it is time to focus on improving our own skills so that we increase our employability. Instead of ranting against politicians on social media, maybe it is better to use social media to improve your networking and further your own career.

The ten-year experiment of trying out various governments and leaders has also taught us one more thing: *nobody is amazing, and nobody is terrible.* There's no point in getting worked up against a particular politician or political party.

Of course, it doesn't come across that way when you log on to your social media. Twitter is flooded with Modi-haters and Rahul-baiters. Both fan clubs relentlessly praise their leader and bash the other. After seeing what has been happening in India for the last ten years, are they seriously deluded, to think one is pure gold while the other one is pure trash? Above all, why are they wasting so much of their own time, energy and passion on such negativity on Twitter? Is it going to boost their careers? Not for most people, unless they are in politics. Is it going to fix all of India's problems? Well, no. So what the hell do they hope to achieve by this passionate time-wasting on politics anyway?

It's hard to convince the social media warriors to change their ways. Maybe it is better to let them stew in their own negativity. However, I want to address *you*, the reader of *this* book. Do not believe in binaries, especially when it comes to politics. Do not expect a particular government to offer solutions to your life's problems. Do not become a negative person. And do not do what is worse: spread more negativity in this already negative world.

The past ten years may have disappointed us, those who dream of India taking its place among the developed nations of the world one day. However, these years have also taught us a lot. Today, rather than talking about what the government is doing wrong, it is time we spoke about we can do right. There's a whole lot of negativity out there. To stand out and shine today, you need to be what I call an 'India Positive Citizen'. I will discuss what it really means to be one on a practical basis in the sections below.

Becoming an India Positive Citizen will, for one, help *you* be a better person and do well in *your* career. But when there are a lot of us who are India positive, we will also help India become a better place and finally create the change we want to see in our country.

An objective, non-partisan look at how we did (2009–2019)

Being India Positive is not a call to be a PR or propaganda agent for India. Far from it. Being India Positive calls for an honest assessment of what we have done right and what we haven't. Neither unnecessarily harsh India-bashing, nor justifying our mistakes or over-praising our country, but an objective look at the achievements and mistakes of the last ten years. Let us examine our performance in both economic and social terms, as summarised in the table below, and discussed in the following section.

India's Performance (2009–2019)		
	Economy overview	Society overview
Where we did really well	Online business boom Startups Better tax compliance and GST	No major regional- or caste-based conflicts Some drop in corruption, fewer scams Decriminalising Section 377 Empowering people with the internet
Where we did okay	GDP growth	Attempts at non-caste, economic-based quotas Some schemes like NREGA, Ujjwala, Jan Dhan and Ayushman increase equality and standard of living
Where we messed up	Missed manufacturing boom Low job creation	Hindu-Muslim polarisation, including lynchings Education system still in shambles

HOW WE DID: ECONOMY

What we did well

India saw a boom in online businesses, in line with the rest of the world, over the past decade. However, given our low internet penetration in 2009, we grew faster than the rest of the world. Data became much cheaper over the last five years, increasing internet usage and thereby boosting online businesses even further. One look at the newspapers around Diwali, and you will see the flood of online shopping ads, something that didn't exist a decade ago. This online boom has also led to a startup culture, with hundreds of angel and venture funds investing in thousands of startups. Many of these startups became unicorns (valued at over a billion dollars). This is one of the true economic achievements of India in the past decade.

We have also seen far higher tax compliance from businesses—whether in terms of income taxes or the GST filings, making Indian businesses far more organised than they were a decade ago.

What we did okay

Estimates vary, but the general consensus is that our GDP grew at a rate of about 8 per cent per year over the past decade. While there are endless debates over which government delivered more growth—the UPA or the NDA—the difference in average numbers over both their terms is small. While India remains one of the fastest-growing economies in the world, this growth rate is not impressive, given our low base and our expectations in 2014. Many expected a stable government with a pro-business mindset to boost economic growth, compared to a coalition government ridden with scams. However, this did not happen. Maybe because of the slowdown due to demonetisation, or because we could not pass crucial land acquisition bills, we were not able to jumpstart our GDP more effectively in 2014–2019 than in the 2009–2014 period. (On the other hand, other countries including China and some South Asian economies, grew in double digits when they were at similar GDP levels as present-day India.) We did okay, but we could have done much better.

Where we messed up

Clearly, the one area where we have not delivered as per need is employment. Barring a tiny percentage of graduates from elite colleges, the youth find it hard to get jobs in our country. It is still possible to hire graduates at ₹10,000 a month, which isn't too different from the situation we had a decade ago. Considering inflation rates, these starting salaries are very low, not to mention the fact that even these jobs are hard to find. While the reasons behind the present employment is a separate discussion, it is quite clear that we have failed in this area.

The other area where India has fallen behind (and this partially explains the scarcity of jobs) is the manufacturing sector. China, a few decades ago, took over the manufacturing operations of the world. This led to factories coming up across China, leading to higher GDP as well as job growth. As China increased its GDP (and labour there became more expensive), we had the perfect opportunity to take over and become the next manufacturing capital of the world. We couldn't. The reasons for this include the failure of the Land Acquisition Bill (early in the NDA government's term), not enough labour reforms, frequent policy changes, the complications of running a business in India, and not enough effort from our side to invite businesses from across the world to set up manufacturing units in India.

HOW WE DID: SOCIETY

What we did well

Social change is as important as economic growth. Again, we did a few things really well. Despite our many differences, the fact that we didn't have major conflicts based on caste and region (religion is a different story, discussed later) during this period is a significant achievement. The rise in internet penetration also means that more Indians are digitally empowered today, creating more equality.

The anti-corruption movement peaked in the last decade, and we have seen a drop in corruption, particularly in high-level scams. For a country like India where corruption is a way of life, this is a major achievement, even though we still have a long way to go.

We also had a landmark ruling when Section 377 was decriminalised by the Supreme Court, marking a major leap in human rights for the LGBTQ community in our country.

Where we did okay

Some major social equality schemes have been initiated in India over the past decade—NREGA, Ujjwala, Ayushman Bharat and the Jan Dhan accounts—all making an impact on our society, to a certain extent. And just recently, a demand was made for introducing non-caste, income-based quotas in the reservation system. The implementation of these quotas is uncertain but it is a step in the right direction.

Where we messed up

Perhaps the one area where we did mess up is in Hindu–Muslim relations. While no large-scale riots occurred in the country in the past decade, there have been terrible incidents of lynchings (including beef-related murders) of members of minority communities. India is divided to begin with, and communal polarisation on various issues has made matters worse. We need to make extra efforts to get people to stick together. Whether it is the BJP's fault or the Congress's, whether you blame the media or social media, the fact is that we are still divided, and there is a long way to go.

Secondly, we have not fixed our broken education system. This makes the already precarious job situation worse. For one thing, most of our students are just not trained well enough to enter the workforce. The number of seats in good colleges has simply not grown at a rapid enough pace to accommodate the increasing number of aspirants for higher education. Many are forced to study abroad. This places huge financial burdens on families of these students, making India lose foreign exchange by draining off the money they could have spent in India instead. Primary education is also not in good shape, the situation being only marginally better than a decade ago.

What can be done to fix all this?

The above analysis is an honest attempt to highlight what India did and didn't do right in the past decade. If we want the next decade to be better, we need to look hard both at where we messed up and at what we did just about okay in. We need to finally do what it takes to increase our GDP in double digits, move the world's manufacturing to India, and create jobs. We need to work harder on Hindu–Muslim relations, and building a less polarised society. Any government that comes next—Congress, BJP or a third-front coalition—will have to work on these issues. We, as citizens, must keep demanding that these things be fixed, no matter who is in power. Hopefully, we will move forward in these areas over the next decade.

What can you do meanwhile: Working on yourself

As discussed above, despite all attempts at change, the needle in India only moves a few points in a decade.

However, come to think of it, a decade is a really short time in the history of a large nation. To expect things to be totally different in ten years is too much. And as we have seen, each government can only accelerate the pace of change so much during its term in power.

However, a decade is a long time when it comes to your own life. If you wait around for policies to change at the top and then percolate down to ultimately change your life, I guarantee you that most of your life will be spent waiting. Hence, yes, we should critically evaluate what we did right or wrong, as a nation. We want India to be run better, and should demand accountability and change. But we should also accept that progress, even in the best of circumstances, will be slow. Meanwhile, since life is short, and we have seen both Congress and BJP in action with their limitations, it is time for us to work on our own lives. All this, while staying objective and positive, and not spreading negativity. Which brings us to what it really means to be a citizen who is India Positive.

What can I do?

To be an India Positive Citizen at a practical level, you must work on these three goals:

1. **Enhance yourself:** A country's biggest asset is its people. Working on your self is the first step towards becoming an India Positive Citizen. The more you educate and improve yourself, the better the country fares. Learn skills that are needed in our society. Computers, good oral and written

communication, understanding how business works, marketing and networking are some of the areas you can work on to enhance your own profile. Instead of watching useless videos, or worse, posting negative comments on social media, use that time to cultivate these skills. An India Positive Citizen will spend most of his or her day upgrading themselves and working towards their goals.

2. **Enhance the nation:** Apart from working on ourselves, being India Positive also means we must try to do a few things that contribute to the nation's welfare. You don't have to become a social worker or activist to be of service to your country. Here are some easy ways:

    a) When you have an income and pay taxes on it, or when you make a purchase and pay the tax on it, you are helping the country.

    b) Refrain from spreading negativity on social media. That alone will help your country. If you can make positive comments, that will help even more. Be solution-oriented rather than criticism-oriented.

    c) Work towards keeping the secular fabric of the nation intact. Make friends from different backgrounds. Don't make divisive statements. Respect the idea of India as a place where a diverse set of people live in peace together.

d) Treat the public spaces of your country as you would your home: don't litter, don't honk, and don't break traffic rules. This simple commitment to civic sense alone, if cultivated by all our citizens, can dramatically change our country in a short period of time.

3. **Remain objective:** The final important aspect of an India Positive Citizen is to be bi-partisan in one's approach to politics when needed. Depending on the situation or the issue in question, you may agree with the Congress or the BJP, the left or the right or any other political party. Let yours be a floating vote. There's no point in lifelong loyalty to any party. If you never change your choices, your vote is no longer a tool of your accountability as a citizen. It is tempting to pledge allegiance to a group as it feels safer to belong. It is lonelier when you are judging things based on realities rather than blind support. However, this objectivity is what the country needs.

If you, the reader, can commit yourself to the above goals, I would consider this book a success. The columns that follow should be read with the same mindset. I have tried to be solution-oriented and objective wherever possible. I hope my take on various issues that affect India resonate with you as well. Come, let us change India together, by being India Positive.

INDIAN SOCIETY, INDIAN CULTURE

For India to truly change, there needs to be a change in our society and culture. The internet is playing a big part in it. The rise of internet penetration also means that things are now more equal, since people who didn't have a voice before now do. 'The Great Opinion Wars talks about how social media has allowed aspirational Indians to voice their opinions on topics that have always been the domain of the privileged class.

However, social media has also birthed a strange new phenomenon in India—the bhakts, and there is advice for both the bhakts and those at the receiving end of their abuse in 'Anatomy of an Internet Troll'. Another phenomenon that social media has caused is 'virtue signallers'—those people who have to show that they are so virtuous, so noble and so good that they sense communal intolerance in a statement even when others don't. 'Look, I'm so Secular!': The Rise of Virtue Signallers on Social Media' talks about this and how it distorts national public debate on a range of important issues.

But do these phenomena indicate that India is getting more intolerant? There are endless debates about this, but I think that we are a mixed society, tolerant and intolerant at the same time, as explained in 'Fifty Shades of Intolerance'. I don't believe that intolerance has anything to do with the request from Hindus that a temple be built in Ayodhya, and 'Why We Need a Ram Temple in Ayodhya' talks about why restoring the temple on its original site and building an even grander mosque nearby will be a great act of religious cooperation.

A crucial aspect of what makes India the country it is, is the fact that we are a democracy, and any attempt to undermine that is dangerous. The essay on blind bhakts talks about how unquestioning support of a leader, rather than the country, can actually harm that leader. The essay on the Supreme Court's order regarding the playing of the national anthem before a movie screening ('Anthem Order: The Intention's Good but Imposition Isn't') argues that authoritarianism can never create patriotism. The government ban on pornography is a similar curtailment of basic freedoms, as explained in 'Hypocritical and Impractical: With the Porn Ban, the Government Has Flaunted Its Control Freak Instincts'. I think that the key to becoming an awesome nation is to defend individual liberties. Related to this is the need to stop mixing religion and law, and 'Too Many Holy Cows' talks about how it is time to discuss what it means to be a secular republic, and revise the Constitution to reflect it.

Social change means that we need to look at the infrastructures in our cities, and the essay on Mumbai rains talks about this and what needs to be done so that the country's financial capital does not come to a grinding halt every monsoon. This overriding indifference that seems to inflict Indians is also reflected on our views on corruption, and our don't-care attitude to corruption is addressed in the essay on the 2G 'non-scam'.

It's important for one to be proud of the country we live in, and 'Will You Spend ₹80 to See India Win a Dozen Olympic Golds?' suggests ways that we can improve our gold medal tally at the Olympics at the micro and macro level.

Finally, 'Creaming the People' suggests a move from caste-based reservations to economic-based ones in order to create a truly fair society.

@chetan_bhagat

Celebrating murder coz victim had opposite ideology is bad. But condemning murders only when the victim's ideology matches yours is also bad

585 replies/ 4,267 retweets/ 9,960 likes

How Blind Bhakts Can Actually Harm India's Democracy

If you are a true nationalist, put the nation before individuals, even if that individual happens to be your favourite leader

I recently conducted a Twitter poll to test the hypothesis that Narendra Modi enjoys an insane amount of support among his fans. The poll asked this question: *If Modi wanted to declare a national emergency to eliminate corruption, would you support it?* Out of nearly 10,000 participants, 57 per cent said they would support such a decision.

The usual Twitter poll disclaimers apply: it's a highly skewed sample, polls aren't scientific, etc. Also, the poll does not indicate my own views in any way, nor does it claim that such a proposal is on the government's anvil. However, the results do give us a sense of what some of Modi's hardcore fans (the bhakts) feel. It is worth noting that the participants were almost all young, educated, digitally savvy people who understand English. Yes, a significant number of progressive young Indians are apparently happy to give up democracy, and vote themselves voteless.

Stunned? Well, I admit that the question was a tad unfair. After all, there is nothing in the air that suggests an emergency is in the offing. Nor does one need to make such harsh choices in order to proclaim their support, or lack of it, for a leader. Still, the numbers do show (a) the enormous popularity of Modi in his core fan base and/ or (b) a possible ignorance of what a national emergency and giving up democracy could mean. They also indicate a huge lack of confidence in the current political system and the kind of leaders it generates.

The reason for Modi's appeal is obvious. After all, he is a leader who has created some hope. He speaks a language that connects us. Modi takes steps—big, bold ones—to fix India. Whether or not they solve problems, is a separate story. Making the effort and having good intentions counts for a lot. Demonetisation is a case in point. Many experts have questioned the benefits of the move. They diligently quote numbers and facts to show that the actual advantages of demonetisation could be marginal. Of course, these are wasted efforts. All this economic mumbo-jumbo is irrelevant to the Modi fan. If fans are ready to support an emergency in their leader's name, do you really think they give a damn about falling GDP or actual data about black money being back in circulation?

No, we are talking about love here. Love doesn't, and is not meant to, see reason. And speaking of demonetisation, the experts, though not wrong, miss a key point. A huge intangible benefit of the note ban has been its unifying effect on an otherwise divided country. Imagine a bickering joint family. One day, the patriarch gets them together to go out and plant trees. They work as a family for a day, and plant a hundred trees. Would you not commend the patriarch for it? Now, imagine that only five of the hundred trees planted by this family survive over time. Would you blame the patriarch? Wouldn't you still give him credit for bringing everyone together for a good cause? This is why many Indians support Modi's demonetisation policy, despite the numbers that point to its ill-effects, whatever they might be.

However, this love does get disturbing when hardcore Modi fans place the individual above the institutions that make India. The interplay of the ruling party, the Opposition and a free media is essential for our democracy. In a state of emergency, this vital balance disappears, leaving our country vulnerable to potentially huge abuses of power. It is a big mistake to think that a messiah will fix India, when in fact it is the political system and societal values that need to be gradually reformed. Countries like Pakistan operate on the messiah principle, falling in love with army generals. We know what a mess such nations have become. Never ever root for the end of democracy, no matter how wonderful your leader might be in your eyes.

In fact, blind faith harms the leader as well as the nation. Today Modi, like any powerful leader, is probably surrounded by yes-men and sycophants. Hardly any of them would have the guts to tell him he is wrong when he makes a mistake. It is from his critics that Modi will learn where he could be going wrong and how to course-correct. This will enable him to formulate policies for the betterment of the country. Considering that our Opposition is in pathetic shape, it is these independent, critical yet constructive voices that form the conscience of Modi-governed India. Blind fans, who will agree to a national emergency if Modi declares it, and are ready to abuse and bully anyone who says anything remotely critical of their idol, are frankly quite useless—to Modi as well as to the nation-building process.

I have little sympathy for elitists, fake liberals and blind Modi-haters. Yet, they are harmless for the most part. However, blind bhakts are worrisome. If you are a true nationalist, put the nation before individuals, even if that individual happens to be your favourite leader. Love your leader by all means, but not more than India and its hard-earned democracy.

Anthem Order: The Intention's Good, but Imposition Isn't

Authoritarianism can never create patriotism, especially when it curtails basic freedoms

Imagine a glass of fresh, health-giving coconut water. But let's say this coconut water has some arsenic mixed in it. You tell people not to drink it. They turn around and say, 'But why are you so against coconut water?'

Or if someone is killed in the name of religion and you object, you are told: 'That just shows you don't love God.'

These examples show what happens when right and wrong are jumbled together. It's a potent, deadly combination. The best way to get away with doing something bad is to mix a bit of good in it. At least, that is what India seems to be witnessing these days.

A case in point is the Supreme Court order that made it 'compulsory' for the national anthem to be played before the screening of every movie in privately owned cinemas across the country, with the doors of the theatres closed (though not bolted). The order also prescribed exactly how the national anthem should be played (with an image of the Indian flag on the screen) and how it should not be played (you can't dramatise it or give it any creative interpretation because, well, the judge said so).

I am no legal expert, but with respect to the apex court, the order did seem to violate the principle of individual liberty, which is protected by our country's Constitution. Ironically, this damage to constitutional values was inflicted in the name of patriotism. The idea was, if people are forced to stand in a cinema hall before a movie, they will become patriotic (watching pirated movies at home, on the other hand, is okay).

Incidentally, when a petitioner tried to get court functionaries to stand up for the national anthem as a rule before they start proceedings, the apex court shot it down. Clearly, it didn't want the burden of patriotism at its doorstep, although it had no qualms about passing it on to privately owned theatres in a private contract with the movie-going public.

These kind of arbitrary rulings are the reason India's ease of doing business rank is so low. Almost anyone in authority can pass such a diktat in the name of the country. If you criticise it, you are asked, 'Why are you against the national anthem?' Worse, you're labelled 'anti-national'.

Which brings us back to the basic issue—mix a bit of good with the bad, and you can get away with it. For instance, the intention to create respect for the country's national anthem at the core of the Supreme Court order cannot be faulted. There is no doubt that every citizen of India should take pride in the national anthem. However, that intention did not justify this imposition.

Sure, one is free to play the national anthem every morning at home and stand up while it's playing.

Institutions such as schools or private companies could choose to make this a daily practice. However, the moment you force it, you break a key tenet of Indian nationalism—individual freedom.

Sadly, the imposition would not have encouraged patriotism. There was a real risk that the young generation would begin to see it merely as a chore that needs to be done if you want to watch a movie at a theatre. Some may have used the time to check messages on their phones. Others may have entered the cinema hall late. Does our national anthem deserve to be trivialised and turned into a tedious task? Should it not be played and sung by people of their own free will and choice? A suggestion or guideline to play the national anthem in public places is welcome, but an imposition is not, as it could threaten the core democratic value of the freedom of the individual.

The order is interim in nature and will be reviewed in February 2017. I respect the Supreme Court and I hope it will reconsider this order.

One should note that this order was issued by the judiciary, and technically has nothing to do with the government or PM Modi. However, it speaks to the somewhat authoritarian mood prevalent in Indian society today—where you are told what to do in order to be a patriot, and may be branded anti-national if you don't fall in line. The reason for this is a weak Opposition, rather than Modi or the BJP. The Congress refuses to get its act together. In Indira Gandhi's time, we saw how a phenomenally weak Opposition created a phenomenally autocratic leader. If we want to save India's free society, let's wish for a strong Opposition. We also need reasonable judges who can preserve the core values that constitute the idea of India.

We should certainly stand up for the national anthem with pride. Equally, however, we should stand up for the freedoms, individual and collective, for which our forefathers gave their lives. We should be careful of authoritarianism creeping into our free society, no matter how wonderful the intentions. Don't condone something bad, just because it is mixed with something good.

---

*Post this article, the Supreme Court modfied the order, stating that the playing of the national anthem in cinema halls is no longer mandatory.

Blame It on the Rain

Till we begin to take responsibility, Mumbaikars will continue to drown in heavy showers

First up, apologies for writing about Mumbai. It is, after all, just one of India's many cities. However, it is also the nation's financial and business capital. The health of this metro has a bearing on the welfare of the rest of the country.

So, it's always worrying when heavy rains bring this supercity to a standstill. For instance, on 2 September 2017, Mumbai received 30 cm of rain in just 24 hours—approximately an eighth of its annual 225 cm average on a single day. This level of precipitation is very high, even though Mumbai has recorded more alarming rainfall data in the past (over 90 cm in a day, in 2005).

Having said that, this is not a level at which the city needs to come to a grinding halt. Yet, when we hit 30 cm, local trains stopped on their flooded tracks. City taxis, aggregator cabs and auto rickshaws alike went off waterlogged roads. Children slept in their schools overnight. Passengers at local train stations parked themselves in abandoned trains, the only dry places they could find, for hours.

The response to this avoidable problem followed a standard pattern. In the morning, the media gushed with praise for the gorgeous spectacle of the Mumbai rains. By noon, pictures of waterlogging flooded social media. A couple of hours later, there were reports of Mumbaikars braving the rain and walking home, embodying the 'unshakeable spirit of Mumbai' (as if the people walking home had any other choice).

Then we had reports of compassion, of Mumbaikars serving hot tea and offering shelter to those stranded on the streets. At night, TV news panellists shouted at each other, as if all the screaming would make the clouds drift away.

Nobody offered any practical solutions. Nobody really knows how things can change for the better. The best hope for Mumbai, which has ramshackle infrastructure even on sunny days, is that God will be kind. Yes, we are a Ram-bharose city.

We may have stock exchange totalling a trillion dollar market capitalisation. We may have civic authorities with billion-dollar budgets. We may have apartments that cost millions of dollars. However, a few hours of rain, and the city collapses.

There is no other major city in the world, which also happens to be a nation's financial capital, with such terrible infrastructure. The local trains are pitiful even on normal days. In many parts of the world, farm animals travel better. Mumbai roads continue to be poorly made, patched up with materials that don't last a single rainy season. The drainage system routinely breaks down in heavy rains.

The authorities care little. Mumbai accounts for only

a tiny percentage of the votes in Maharashtra, and lacks political clout despite its high profile. Add to this the apathy of its people, who gather in lakhs if their religious sentiments or their guru are insulted, but won't do the same to improve basic amenities in their city.

If angry Mumbaikars come out on the streets in large numbers for just one day and demand 'fix my city', the authorities will sit up and take notice. We don't. Instead, we prefer to retweet helpline numbers and share stories of those who offered chai to people stranded by the rains. Well, we get the city we deserve.

Meanwhile, here are two suggestions that will help—not just Mumbai, but other Indian cities as well. The first is easy and should be implemented as soon as possible. The second is harder, but will truly fix the problem. It is up to the authorities to implement these and the citizens to put pressure on them to do the same.

One, we urgently need an effective weather warning system. Weather reports saying 'heavy rains expected' aren't likely to help citizens take necessary precautions. There has to be a scale which informs people precisely how bad the weather is likely to get, and what actions need to be taken at each level. For instance, the scale could be as follows: 0: Normal situation; 1: Weather may deteriorate, keep watching weather reports; 2: Strong rains/winds, primary schools to be closed; 3: Very strong rains/winds, all schools to be closed, advise others to stay home; 4: Extremely bad weather, all schools, colleges, and offices to be closed, essential services only, limited public transport, stay indoors; 5: Entire city shutdown.

A good warning system could help people plan their movements, dramatically reducing hardship in bad weather. For instance, 2 September would have been a '4'; in 2005, we had a '5'.

A weather warning system like the above is similar to the typhoon signal system in Hong Kong, which works brilliantly. Hong Kong also receives heavy rain; however, the city doesn't suffer or stall as much in bad weather.

Of course, predicting weather is difficult, despite advances in technology. There may be intermittent false alarms. However, the loss in productivity caused by these would be limited, as technology has also made it possible for people to work from home on occasion.

The second suggestion is to improve the roads. Coal tar is nothing more than a coat of paint. It erodes over months, leaving potholes. All new Mumbai roads must be made of cement, by law. Roads in Mumbai need to be made of cement and concrete, as in several developed countries, or even in parts of Lutyens' Delhi, and the use of these materials in road-building needs to be enforced by law. A world-class drainage system is equally necessary. And yeah, it would be nice if the people involved didn't steal public money.

Mumbai has suffered enough. It is time we stopped accepting this suffering, or worse, celebrating it. Excess rainfall is tough to handle in a big city. But with the right weather warning systems, good roads and effective drainage, it need not cripple Mumbai. It is time we fixed the city.

@chetan_bhagat

So the financial capital of the world's biggest democracy and a major economy shuts down again in less than a month, because, well it rained.

195 replies/ 422 retweets/ 2,876 likes

@chetan_bhagat

Banning crackers on Diwali is like banning Christmas
trees on Christmas and goats on Bakr-Eid. Regulate.
Don't ban. Respect traditions.

2,165 replies/ 8,348 retweets/ 15,417 likes

Why We Need a Ram Temple in Ayodhya

Restoring the temple on its original site and building an even grander mosque nearby will be a great act of religious cooperation

It has become the fashion in some elite Indian circles to bash Hinduism, or issues related to it. It has also been taboo in these same intellectual circles to discuss what I think is a very reasonable request—that we should have a Ram temple in Ayodhya. The elite, particularly in the English media, have bullied almost all voices that desire a temple at the sacred site into silence.

Hence, just to be clear, I would like to state this: peacefully, but definitely, I support the construction of a beautiful Ram temple in Ayodhya. It is frankly ridiculous that we have to beg to restore a temple at one of Hinduism's greatest sites.

Of course, something needs to be clarified here. Violence in any form, including the kind that happened in 1992, cannot be supported. It was wrong, illegal and unfortunate, and should never happen again.

However, this does not take away the reasonableness of the request to restore a place of worship in one of the holiest sites of the Hindu religion. This article seeks to make a case for a temple in Ayodhya and debunk the various theories that have prevented its construction all these years.

The first argument against the temple is 'why disturb the status quo?' Its proponents say that there is a dormant issue at stake, and building a temple would risk destroying the peace. Well, there is no reason why peace should be disturbed by such a project in the first place.

I think the Muslim community, or the various leaders that claim to represent it, should give its blessing to the temple in any case. This is no ordinary site. As per Hindu faith, Ayodhya is the birthplace of Lord Rama, one of the most revered gods in the pantheon. Diwali is India's biggest festival.

Thousands of mosques stand on erstwhile temple sites in India, courtesy the Mughal rulers. Nobody is asking for these temples to be restored. But this is Lord Rama's birthplace, replaced by yet another mosque. The mosque can be shifted. The holy site of Lord Rama's birthplace is a matter of centuries of faith. We can't shift that.

A grander mosque can be built nearby, or even right next door. Why won't the Muslim community accommodate such a reasonable appeal? Is it because some of their self-styled leaders are politically instigated to do the opposite? I am sure the general Muslim population of this country would approve such a request. We just need to approach them directly. And in the age of social media, we can.

'Build a hospital instead' is the second kind of argument made against the building of the temple. We need more hospitals, yes, but they don't have to be built on this site! Hospitals can be constructed on any piece of land, and should be located based on where people need them most. Why on such a holy site? Frankly, why can't we make a Ram temple at the site as well as a great hospital somewhere else?

The third argument against the temple is: 'But God is everywhere, so why here?' Or: 'But what is the proof Lord Rama was born here?' True, God is everywhere. But we still need places of worship. So that when we visit these sites, we can focus on God and God alone. As far as conclusive proof of the site in Ayodhya being the place of Lord Rama's birth goes, there is none. But we do have proof that this site has been known as the birthplace of Lord Rama for centuries, and excavations have shown that there was a temple here before the mosque was built.

India is a nation that respects all religions. To prove that, sometimes we tend to become extra sensitive to the grievances of religious minorities, but often ignore any issues the majority religion may have. The Ram temple is an example. Previous governments, particularly, have made it a policy to appease minorities, to the extent that even reasonable requests have been made to look like majoritarian bullying.

This temple could be a symbol of understanding between the two dominant religious communities of India. Neither restoring a temple on its original site nor shifting a mosque to a nearby location (and making it grander) tarnishes the glory of Islam in any manner. In fact, the surge in tourism that the project will create in

Ayodhya once it is completed, will generate jobs for both Hindus and Muslims.

The only thing we have to ensure is to keep a lid on any form of incitement to communal violence this project may create. Today, in the age of better digital communication, these risks are minimal. This is a request from the Hindu community at large to the Muslim community at large, and the elites and the intellectuals of this country—let us have our temple. Bless its restoration and the building of a grander mosque nearby, so that we can peacefully create one of the greatest sites of religious cooperation in the whole world.

The Great Opinion Wars

Privileged influencers and aspirational India are locked in a battle to mould opinion

We think an elected government in power can do anything it wants. However, the government of the day, or for that matter most political leaders, almost always act on the basis of current public opinion.

There are always a few opinion leaders and influencers, both individuals and entities (such as the media) with disproportionate influence on public thought and opinion. Most citizens form their views based on the influencers they trust, or in most cases don't form a view at all. They are happy to vote once every five years and let the country be run by people in power, guided by these makers of public opinion.

This is how India works too, with one added peculiarity. Public opinion in our country has almost always been in the hands of the privileged class. The most obvious marker of belonging to this class is good spoken English, along with some or all of the following: a) access to good private English-medium schools; b) access to higher education in a prestigious liberal arts college; c) growing up in a metro city; d) growing up in an upper middle class household; e) connections with other members of this privileged class; and f) getting a job because you know someone, rather than through merit. India's privileged classes are eloquent; they speak and write well, and can generally express themselves better than others. Naturally, they are a good fit for the role of opinion leaders.

Ever since the British Raj, these intellectuals have told the hoi polloi what to think. They controlled opinion on every issue: whether it was Kashmir, minorities, economic policies or women's rights. Often, they tended to be left-leaning in their politics. This was understandable. Success in a capitalist society depends on individual merit. To someone in a position of privilege, such a system can be a huge threat.

The new millennium changed all that. India and Indians grew in economic power. Many citizens aspired to bigger goals. And they wanted, god forbid, a say in how the country was run too. Not just at election time (where they elected Modi, replacing privileged dynasts), but also on a daily basis.

Technology such as social media increasingly allows them to do so. You needn't hold a certain degree from a particular college to have an opinion on Kashmir. You could simply be a thinking Indian and you qualify. If your opinion resonates, it will circulate and influence others.

Of course, this scared the privileged class. They fought back, calling capitalists Sanghis and nationalists Hindu zealots. Aspirational India fought back too, calling the privileged class fake liberals and 'presstitutes'.

This battle for opinion is in full swing in India today.

Almost all the recent big controversies—award wapsi, tolerance/intolerance, national/anti-national and the recent India–Pakistan relationship shift—are instances of the Great Indian Opinion Wars.

The privileged classes still have enormous clout. For instance, look at the furore the English news channels make, and the number of politicians who react to them. In fact, the viewership of the leading Hindi news channels can be a hundred times that of the English channels. Yet, the English media continues to control opinion. Similarly, Indian intellectuals who write in English are more influential. The international media reacts almost solely to them.

Meanwhile, the battle continues. As aspirational India rises, it clamours to have its say, though it often does so in noisy, sentimental and even crass terms. These new opinion-makers may have merit in their thoughts, but they often lack rationality or eloquence of expression. They want Pakistanis out. They want respect for their traditions, like the beef-eating taboo. They want a strong leader who takes action against terrorism, regardless of consequences. They want nationalism.

The aspirational set may have sense on their side. However, they can't logically or persuasively explain their views as well as the privileged set can. They compensate by showing strength in numbers and shoving opinions down people's throats. In other words, they often behave like a mob.

Not long ago, many supported a ban on an Indian film that had cast a Pakistani actor. This happened at a time when India had sent peace missions to Pakistan. It's an instance of how things could go wrong if the aspirational class replaces the privileged class.

The privileged class is responsible for a lot of wrongs. They are disconnected from reality, monopolise opinion, and have led India into poverty with their left-leaning ideas, nepotism and disregard for true merit. However, this doesn't mean we can replace them with the mob. It doesn't mean we can disregard laws, logic, politeness, open-mindedness and individual liberties in the name of nationalism. The true Indian patriot is someone who loves this nation, and has respect for the law as well as the differences in opinion that may exist in a free country.

Labelling people 'anti-national' for not agreeing with you is not going to help. Instead, demolish those who hold a different view with a polite but strong counter-argument. Patriotic emotion is a good thing, but logical thoughts are also necessary if you want a say in public opinion.

Privileged classes and the new aspirational India need to learn to coexist with each other. The old elite need to understand the new reality where privilege no longer gives you instant entitlement or a monopoly over public opinion. Aspirational India has to learn to articulate and conduct itself well, and remain open-minded to others. In the Great Indian Opinion Wars, may the best opinion for India win, whichever side it comes from.

Too Many Holy Cows: Let's Just Stop Mixing Religion and Law

The law of the land should resist the influence of religion-specific codes and directives

Before I begin, let me confirm that I am a Hindu. I don't eat beef. Now, I consider myself a fairly rational person. However, some of my reasons for not eating beef don't have a scientific basis. My religion tells me that the cow must be revered. So I avoid cow meat in my diet. Yet, I wear leather shoes, watch cricket matches that use leather balls and drink cow's milk taken against the animal's consent. Many other Hindus do the same. I eat chicken and lamb burgers. But I won't eat a beef burger. It may not exactly make sense. It's 'just one of those things'; the religious practices we adhere to out of faith in our rituals, traditions and culture.

Hinduism is not the only religion with taboos and prohibitions. Islam prohibits the eating of pork. It prescribes that an animal be slaughtered in a certain manner if its meat is to be consumed by believers. Jews don't eat dairy and meat products at the same time. Once again, all these practices belong to the category of 'just one of those things'. There is no point in trying to find logical flaws in them. They exist since millions of people follow them, and they seem to add some positive value to their lives.

In theocratic states, religion forms the basis of law. Right or wrong, logical or illogical, citizens of such states have to abide by these rules. Some of these might well be 'just one of those things'. However, if you break them, you break the state's law. And you could face criminal prosecution for it. Several Islamic states around the world are examples. In such countries, individuals enjoy less freedom, as religion can't be questioned by rational thought. To many Indians, this would be a huge setback to the quality of their lives. Freedom is precious to us. It's who we are.

Thankfully, and quite remarkably, the people who drafted our Constitution designed India as a secular republic. Despite a majority Hindu population and a violent partition that led to the creation of a separate Islamic state, the architects of our nation had vision. They did not cave in and turn India into a Hindu state. The Indian Constitution has several provisions that protect and treat all religions as equal.

However, the drafters of our Constitution also made a few provisions, perhaps for good reason, that slanted towards the beliefs of a particular religion. This included Article 48, a directive that asks states to protect cows from slaughter. Yes, 'one of those things' made it into the Constitution of a secular republic. So did a few other practices. The fact that different religions follow different civil codes meant that certain laws in our country were opposed to the principle of equality. This made it possible under law for a Muslim man to have four wives, for instance, or to divorce his wife with an oral proclamation.

Why did the drafters of the Constitution make these exceptions? Perhaps, in creating a secular republic, a relatively alien idea then, they didn't want to antagonise various religious groups and jeopardise the whole process. Hence, Indian secularism became not only about treating all religions equally but also about protecting existing religious practices. So far so good.

The problem arose when the Indian Constitution contradicted itself. For its idea of the fundamental rights of its citizens entitles them to live in a free manner. Hence the restriction on beef, a common food item worldwide, is an issue. Similarly, Muslim marriage laws that favour men contradict the right to equality of Muslim women. These fissures remain in the Constitution. Politicians are quick to exploit the hostilities and differences already existing between communities for handles to drag religion into politics.

If we really want to solve problems like the beef question, we need to discuss the broader issue. What direction should we move in as a nation? Should we work towards a common civil code and avoid the 'one of those things' laws that come from specific religions? Or should we keep some of these laws to avoid offending certain groups? I'd like the former to happen. So would many others. However, we also don't want to force a modern code on traditional people so fast that they just reject it and rebel. In some countries, imposing laws against the will of the people has even led to civil wars. On the other hand, if we allow every 'one of those things' to creep into our law books, rationality and logic will vanish.

Obviously, the Dadri incident was deplorable. Mob killings must be condemned and the law of the land upheld. Yet, according to the law in Uttar Pradesh (and many other states), you could be jailed for killing a cow or eating its meat. And the law comes from a directive of the Indian Constitution, which in turn comes from a Hindu religious practice. Even if Dadri hadn't happened, does this law seem right?

We could discuss abolishing the laws that prohibit cow slaughter. But there is a caveat. If we only remove this law and let all the laws that protect Islamic beliefs and practices remain, it will be grossly unfair. Let political parties and religious heads decide to remove all religion-specific laws from our law books. Let us educate people about why it is important to do so. What we see instead is cacophony, posturing and a lot of finger-pointing as political parties whip up controversies to secure their respective vote banks.

The time has come to discuss the idea of a secular republic again, and revise the Constitution to reflect it. It is time we separated governance from 'those things'. For history tells us nothing good is ever likely to come of mixing religion and law.

@chetan_bhagat

Instead of obsessing about linking Aadhar card with PAN card, can we link Dalits to non-Dalits, Muslims to Hindus and Indians to Indians first.

1,792 replies/ 5,536 retweets/ 24,542 likes

Creaming the People: Caste-based Reservations Need to Be Recast for the Sake of a More Just Society

Income-based criteria should replace caste-based ones in our reservation system

In India, we tend to stay away from certain issues in the name of political correctness. Sadly, those are often the ones that most need attention. One such contentious issue in our society is caste-based reservations. While this is often a dormant concern in people's minds, it takes little provocation for the issue to flare up over and over again. The Patel community protests in Gujarat are an example. They attracted so many people that the state government had to ban internet and SMS services to contain the wildfire. And while the protests may have stopped spilling onto the streets for now, the issue remains in people's hearts.

You cannot ban the internet every time a protest breaks out. If at all the Patel agitation taught us a lesson, it is that the current reservation policy, although formulated with good intentions, needs a relook. This is exactly what RSS supremo Mohan Bhagwat suggested when he asked for a review of existing reservation policies with a view to making them fairer. Of course, his comment was seen as a political blunder, as it might help consolidate the anti-BJP Dalit vote in Bihar. Hence it is no surprise that nobody from the BJP or any other major political party actually concurred with Bhagwat's view.

However, we must factor in the long-term interest of the nation. We must have a reservation policy that best achieves its primary objective—to build a more just and equal society. We must also accept that reservation is a shortcut. It is a stopgap, an artificial (albeit quick) way to bring about social equality. It doesn't create opportunity. It simply takes opportunity from someone who is deserving and hands it to another, purely on the basis of their caste affiliation at birth. In doing so, it divides society, fosters mediocrity and demotivates the talented. Hence, reservation is not victimless; it is achieved at a cost to society.

Around 50 per cent of the seats in central government educational institutions as well as government job placements is reserved for Other Backward Castes (OBC), Scheduled Castes (SC) and Scheduled Tribes (ST). Among OBCs, the concept of the creamy layer applies: families with an annual income of more than ₹6 lakh are not eligible for reservation benefits. This does not apply to SCs and STs.

Historically, and in parts of India even to this day, people from backward castes have been discriminated against and denied opportunities. However, this sentence was true even in, say, 1965. Has nothing changed in the last fifty years? Haven't the reservation policies, which were meant to create a fairer society, achieved their goal to a certain extent? Of course, things have changed.

A National Commission for Scheduled Castes and
Scheduled Tribes study reveals that SC candidates alone
comprised only around 1 per cent of Class I (the more
elite) government jobs in 1965. This share had increased
to 10 per cent by 1995. The number is probably even
higher today.

This dramatic rise in numbers of people from
backward communities in top government jobs shows
that the reservation policy has been successful. However,
do note that children of these high-grade SC/ST officers
also get reservation benefits. This feudal upper class
within the SC and ST categories will inherit the benefits
of growing up in an affluent environment from their
parents and still be eligible for a quota of seats or jobs
like any other below-poverty-line SC/ST candidate.

The cream in the creamy layer is only going to get
thicker, denying benefits to the truly needy. The solution
lies in linking reservation benefits to something more
quantifiable as an indicator of denied opportunity:
income. The annual income of a household is a pretty
good indicator of whether a child in that house would
have had the same opportunities and resources to study
for an IIT or IAS entrance exam as a middle or upper
class child. As a yardstick for reservation, it seems fair.
And today, technology allows us to measure, track and
monitor household income like never before.

What is wonderful about basing the system on
economic criteria is this: as per capita incomes rise, the
pool of people eligible for reservation will automatically

shrink. We may even see a day when we won't need reservation at all.

Imagine an India where your caste was irrelevant, and only your talent mattered. If you were born to a poor family, you would get the necessary support to develop your talent. That seems like a much fairer system than the one which prevails now, where some castes get reservation, and so-called upper castes kill themselves to fight for the leftover seats.

Some argue that reservation is not only for economic upliftment but also works towards emancipating the social status of a caste. But wouldn't it be a better solution to eliminate the caste system altogether? Don't bring the issue into governance. Let society look down on people who enquire about someone else's caste for any purpose at all. If it is illegal in our country to make disparaging comments about people from the Northeast or backward castes, why not make it illegal to talk about caste altogether?

Most of the world operates very well without caste. Surnames are just names; they don't have to place you in society. What use is the caste system today anyway? A lot has changed and the time has come to recast reservations, using fresh criteria and modern technology. If we don't do it, the youth that this system steals opportunities from in the name of justice won't forget it. You don't create fairness by doing something unfair.

Hypocritical and Impractical: With the Porn Ban, the Government Has Flaunted Its Control Freak Instincts

Instead of policing the private lives of citizens with needless bans, the government should pay attention to basic reforms in key sectors

First of all, let me say that it isn't easy to take a stance against something like a ban on pornography. We are a hypocritical society, especially so in matters related to sex. Yet, it is safe to assume that most men and several women in our country consume pornography. However, few Indians can admit to this, leave alone come out publicly against the ban.

However, the purpose of this article is not to defend pornography. Porn can, in some instances, have harmful effects. Overexposure to porn can desensitise and degrade one's attitude to sex, harm one's ability to form intimate relationships, encourage objectification of women and lead to motivation and self-confidence issues.

That said, over one-fifth of the world's internet traffic is porn. It is clearly a mass product consumed by billions across the globe, satisfying some basic and regular needs. And a majority of its consumers seem to be going about their lives in a fairly normal manner.

Morally, legally, socially, politically and practically, a ban on porn makes no sense at all in a free society.

The arguments that I am about to make on these five counts should be seen not as encouragement to watch porn, but to understand why we should avoid arbitrary state-mandated bans.

Morally, we in India have a negative attitude towards sex or any form of sexual pleasure. In common Indian parlance, for instance, 'bura kaam' and 'gandi baat' ('bad' or 'dirty' thing) are popular euphemisms for sex. Hence, it is no surprise that proponents of the ban view anything related to porn with fear and disgust.

The same attitude explains several Indian men's attitude towards sex. In my experience, I have yet to meet an Indian girl who has not been leered at, brushed against, groped, molested or made uncomfortable while she was growing up. Brutal rapes might be rare, but no Indian woman is spared unwanted advances from Indian men. That is what needs to be banned.

Sex isn't bad. Non-consensual sex is. There is no 'buri baat' in two consenting adults having sex. But it is a 'buri baat' if a man brushes past a woman in a train or a bus to get a cheap thrill. Preventing people from watching a movie, in the privacy of their homes, about adults having consensual sex, however, won't solve this problem. In fact, it is immoral to interfere in other people's private lives.

Legally speaking, Article 21 of the Indian Constitution lays emphasis on individual freedom. Telling people what not to watch seems to be a clear violation of this principle. Sure, some of our more archaic laws may be cited to support this, but do we have to? Do we have to impose a regressive, control-freak legal regime?

The argument that porn is detrimental to social welfare is also specious. Sexual frustration amongst Indian men is enormous, partly because our so-called Indian culture denies natural instincts and calls for their repression. This could be one of the factors that leads to uncles molesting nieces, and women being groped in buses or trains. Porn may reduce some of that frustration and prevent repression from spilling out in our households and on our streets. Banning porn will increase frustration levels and make crimes against women worse. Do we really want more hidden cameras in trial rooms?

Politically too, the ban is not a wise move. The BJP loves pleasing its most regressive and orthodox constituency which is also perhaps the most loyal. However, it is the new, more progressive generation that helped them come to power. It is likely that a good percentage of the younger BJP supporters on social media watch porn. To deny them this choice of recreation is only going to make the party unpopular.

Finally, at a practical level, even if you want to, you cannot ban porn by blocking websites. I remember VHS days—porn was rampant even when the internet did not exist. You block some sites, and mirror sites pop up or porn gets sold at mobile repair shops in memory cards at every street corner. It's idiotic to believe that a ban on porn can actually be implemented.

A question that arises from all arguments around bans is this: should anything ever be banned? The answer is simple. Certain things that cause immediate and grave harm to society have to be banned or criminalised. A drug like heroin, for instance, can destroy families quickly. A perversion like child pornography, which by definition is criminal activity because it involves children below the age of consent, should clearly be banned.

We need to grow up if we want the world to take us seriously. The key to becoming an awesome nation is to defend individual liberties. India needs to believe that its citizens are not stupid and can choose what is best for them in the right quantity. A republic of bans assumes people are inept and unable to choose, so the state has to decide for them. When a state doesn't believe in its own people, what hope is there for the world to believe in us?

Rather than policing the private lives of citizens, the government should invest its time in increasing our GDP, maintaining law and order, and improving basic education, healthcare and infrastructure in the country. Yes, protect us from crime and substances that will kill us or exploit our children. However, for the rest, believe that people have the right to choose. After all, it is the same right that brought this government to power. So believe in the power of that choice, not in bans.

@chetan_bhagat

If you are a true Indian citizen, make a choice during elections but then keep all parties accountable on real issues, even the one you voted for. If you are a troll, vote and side with one party and keep screaming in their defense all day long on twitter.

193 replies/ 327 retweets/ 2,039 likes

Anatomy of an Internet Troll

How social media birthed a strange new phenomenon in India: the bhakts

The rise of the internet and social media has led to a strange new discovery in India. It is the strong and distinctive presence of a cyber-species often referred to as 'bhakts'. The term is used to refer to owners of right-wing user accounts who tend to be aggressive fans of all things Hindu.

Politically, they often lend their support to BJP, seen as a somewhat pro-Hindu organisation. They are extremely protective of Prime Minister Narendra Modi. They also like old Hindu kings and conspiracy theories about how Hindus were short-changed in the past, often swapping such stories online.

These bhakts would have been a truly interesting anthropological phenomenon, had it not been for the distress they cause from time to time on Twitter. A few years ago, journalist Sagarika Ghose coined the term 'Internet Hindus' to describe them when they attacked her online. Another instance was when the true bhakt species targeted outspoken women on Twitter who didn't think much of the rather sweet and harmless 'selfie with daughter' campaign that was backed by the PM.

So, who are these true bhakts? What drives them? And what can we do to calm them down? More importantly, what can they do? To answer this, it is important to try and understand them.

For one thing, these true bhakts are not just all Hindu fanatics or VHP members. Some of them don't even identify with the Hindu cause; they call themselves nationalists instead. Their stated aim, if you are to believe them, is nation-building and winning back for India its lost glory.

In reality, they are neither Hindu warriors nor nationalists. Typically, and at the risk of stereotyping them, true bhakts have the following traits in common. First, they are almost all male. Second, they have weak communication skills, particularly in English. Such individuals often nurse an inferiority complex about not being cool or sophisticated enough in a fast-changing, globalising world.

Third, they are generally not good at talking to women. As a result, they are unlikely to know how to behave with them or woo them. They fail to attract the women they desire. In other words, if I may say so, this type of individual tends to be sexually frustrated.

Fourth, there is an overriding sense of shame about being Hindu, Hindi-speaking and/or Indian. Deep down, they know that Hindi-speaking Hindus are among India's poorest. They also know that India is a Third World country with third-rate infrastructure and few achievements on the world stage in the fields of science, sports, military technology or art.

To hide this shame, they overcompensate in terms of chest-thumping nationalism. Also, in their minds, the BJP leaders and Modi in particular are the highest aspirational figures. Modi unabashedly identifies with the Hindi/Hindu/modest-means background they belong to, and represents the best people like them can aspire to be.

Modi's success gives true bhakts a genuine reason to rejoice and feel that they too can rise to the top. Hence, protecting his image is of vital importance to them. So, you see true bhakts defending Modi's silence on various scams and vigorously attacking anyone who questions or criticises the PM. Objectivity is lost when people see and worship a leader as an idealisation of their own kind.

Hence, any inferiority-complex-ridden Indian male who is sexually frustrated, ashamed of his background and has poor ability to communicate in English is liable to transform into a true bhakt. And that's why confident, English-speaking women who oppose Modi hit a raw nerve on all counts, getting the worst of the true bhakt treatment.

Since social media offers anonymity, their anger often takes the form of the worst kind of personal abuse. Note that the BJP never invited these true bhakts to worship them. In fact, the PM had to tell them off, as even he seems to have had enough of their hyper-aggressive bhakti.

Of course, at the end of the day, easy votes are welcome and the BJP doesn't mind where they're coming from. However, the party must distance itself from unrestrained testosterone. This kind of support makes it look pretty unsavoury and cements its hard-line image.

Ultimately, the Indian voter will get scared and go back to their default party—the Congress. There's a reason they ruled the country for sixty years and the BJP has just about made eight.

Meanwhile, what can we do? The best strategy is to not take true bhakts too seriously. Of course, it is difficult to ignore personal abuse on social media. But try to understand their motivations. They are not Modi bhakts; they are simply Frustrated And Complex-ridden Indian Males (FACIMs, pronounced fai-kims, not to be confused with the curse word you may want to use on them). Of course FACIM doesn't have the same ring to it as 'bhakt', but it is a more accurate descriptor.

To FACIMs themselves, I would say only this. Smarten up, learn English and practise it. Make some female friends and ask their advice on how to talk to a girl. When you're feeling confident enough, try to ask a woman out and date her like a gentleman. Who knows, you may get lucky soon. Once you do, trust me, you will have better things to do than abuse people on Twitter. Good luck!

What the 2G Non-scam Tells Us About India's Don't-care Attitude to Corruption

We need to focus on the real problems that afflict the nation, and resist media manipulation of non-issues into controversies

The 2G-scam is now officially a 2G non-scam, according to the court. This article will address it as such, and try to figure out why we have so many 'non-scams' in our country.

Spectrum, unlike cow fodder or artillery guns, does not physically exist. You can't touch it, keep it in your pocket or lock it up in a safe. It exists in thin air, a range of invisible waves, and should be available for all to use. However, governments around the world restrict and sell spectrum use rights to telecom companies which transmit calls and data between millions of individual users like you and me.

Selling mobile phone spectrum, hence, is a pretty neat way for the government to make money out of thin air. This is fine as long as the money is used for the welfare of the people. The problem arises when licences are granted to some at a friends-and-family discount, foregoing what a competitive auction would generate.

Of course, no politician does this in a blatant manner. Friends and family are always favoured in subtle but effective ways. For instance, you can bring a licence application deadline forward and tell only your friends about it. Or, you can use a first-come-first-serve process instead of an auction. All this happened in the 2G non-scam.

What also happened was that many such friends flipped and resold their licences (masking them as corporate Mergers & Acquisitions deals, of course) for five to ten times more than what they paid for them, within months. Many thought this was sufficient proof that favours were done.

Hence, for a while, it did seem like a scam. The CAG went wild, stating a loss-to-exchequer figure so big it wouldn't fit in a normal calculator. The Supreme Court found this family-and-friends-discount offer repulsive and cancelled all 122 licences. The media went crazy. Even the PM at the time softly called such events 'coalition compromises'. Enraged people used their new smartphones, and the same tainted spectrum, to post their anger on social media. Some hit the streets. The government lost the next election. A chief minister became the new prime minister, and for many, a saviour who would rid India of all this corruption.

However, the court has now said 'there is no scam'. The accused have been acquitted. The new government-controlled CBI could not find evidence at all. Meanwhile, we Indians were left scratching our heads and wondering, 'What happened? Are we idiots?'

What happened was this. We stopped caring about corruption. We cared about it from 2010 to 2014, when we expressed it on social media, the streets and, finally, EVMs. After that, we had vented enough and we were done. Then we did what we do best—started worshipping or hating a leader, cared about irrelevant issues such as caste/cows/religion far more than governance, and stayed as divided as we can be.

So, imagine you are a politician. And you know people care about silly issues like cows or a *Padmavati* release far more than difficult issues like how our courts handle scams. What would you do? Won't it be simpler to let people discuss cows?

This is the bitter truth about us Indians: we don't care so much about corruption. Some politician stole some money a while back? Oh well, that's what they do, who cares? Any random, irrelevant Hindu–Muslim issue? Oh yes, bring it on. Tell me about that love-jihad couple again?

We get the governance we deserve. That is why we don't have a good follow-through mechanism for scams (or non-scams). Sometimes, when corruption reaches crazy proportions, it does bother us. However, our worry is transient, like a sneeze. We express anger, and we are done. Now we can go back to ranting about cows being disrespected.

It is the court that has decided 2G is a non-scam, not the government, some might argue. However, the task of providing evidence was in the hands of the CBI, a government entity. It was never going to be easy. Corruption is no longer blatant or overt, with clear money exchanges. It is increasingly done in a subtle manner. A rule bent here, a favour granted there, and the reward given at some later date in some other form. Only if public pressure is intense and sustained does any government keep corruption on top of the priority list. The 2G non-scam is a clear example of what happens when citizens don't have their values and priorities in the right place.

So what is more important to you? The resolution of a scam that cost your country billions, or the Muslim boy who ran away with a Hindu girl last week? Our collective answer will decide how many more non-scams we shall see in the near future in our country.

@chetan_bhagat

Screaming about corruption and proving it in court are two different things. **#2GVerdict**

143 replies/ 308 retweets/ 1,950 likes

@chetan_bhagat

Modi haters be like: Hater: You are scared to speak on
fuel prices in Modi regime
Me: I just did that
Hater: No u didn't do it with as much anger
Me: Ok, am really upset
Hater: Ok abuse Modi now, like really badly
Me: well why should I?
Hater: see...bhakt bhakt bhakt!

1,671 replies/ 7,606 retweets/ 28,731 likes

'Look, I'm So Secular!': The Rise of Virtue Signallers on Social Media

The rising trend of virtue signalling on social media risks distorting rational public debate on a range of important issues

The rise of social media in the past few years has meant that public opinion is debated, discussed and shaped on forums like Twitter and Facebook, as well as thousands of local WhatsApp groups. One would imagine these powerful tools that connect millions enable us to distil the best opinions on an issue, which in turn shape our response to them.

However, there is a huge problem. These discussion forums are public. And in public, a lot of people are fake. They want to be seen as good, proper, balanced, modern and progressive. Most of all, they want to be seen as virtuous. In other words, if I can come across as a person who has these wonderful qualities to my 200-odd Facebook, Twitter or WhatsApp friends, it is more valuable than actually saying what I feel on the issue.

In this context, a term called 'virtue signalling' has become popular on the internet recently, although it was first used in a few articles that appeared several years ago. But it is only now that you see virtue signalling on full display.

Try this. Mention that 'I don't feel safe sending my parents on the Amarnath Yatra after Muslim terrorists killed Hindu pilgrims.' Chances are that several people out there will scream 'Communal! Communal!' at your statement before you even understand what on earth happened.

Of course, there is nothing wrong in your original statement, which expresses a fear based on an actual incident that has occurred. You see, these people have to show that they are so virtuous, so noble and so good that they sense communal intolerance in a statement even when others don't.

This virtuous lot on the internet will demand a) that you don't mention any religion at all, b) that Hindus, being a majority, must never raise an issue that affects Hindus because that makes us majoritarians, and c) that a truly virtuous person will not see this as an act against Hindus, but merely as a matter of some bad people trying to hurt good people, and that is all that needs to be said.

Of course, that is not how the human mind works or thinks. The fact remains that many Hindus will now think twice about sending their elderly parents to pilgrimage sites, particularly in Kashmir. Unsavoury though this fact may be, it needs to be discussed. How can we live in a country where people feel unsafe about going to their places of worship? Does discussing this issue in order to come up with solutions spread communal hatred?

According to the virtue signallers, it does. Your mentioning the word 'Hindu', let alone talking about an issue that affects only Hindus, will brand you as a communalist. And by labelling you as such, they come across as virtuous. And when they attack you online, they are saying, 'Look, I am such a secular person that the mere mention of the word "Hindu" makes me mad. Look, I am so good and secular that any hint of a Hindu issue makes me seethe with anger. And now that I have shown I am more virtuous, I have the right to attack others. My goodness gives me sanction to abuse, insult and be rude to anyone else who isn't that virtuous.'

We sometimes mistakenly refer to these people in India as fake-liberals, pseudo-seculars or elitists. In fact, all they are doing is virtue signalling, showing how modern and progressive they are—so that they look good to their virtual peers.

Take a statement like, 'Although we must have laws to protect women, some men suffer due to fake domestic violence or harassment charges because these laws can be abused (something any lawyer or policeman dealing with such cases will attest to).' Virtue signallers will pounce on this and feast all day, calling it 'sexist, anti-women, backward' or whatever else, because they have to show that they are more conscious of gender equality than anyone else.

Virtue signallers operate in many other arenas. They show support for women's cricket in their social media feed though chances are that they have never watched a women's cricket match on TV in their lives. They also want to promote independent cinema over commercial cinema, though in all likelihood they have never watched an independent film in a theatre. Virtue signallers want to demonstrate that they care about Dalits and Muslims, not because they actually care about Dalits and Muslims or do anything about their issues, but because saying so makes you look good on social media.

Beware of such utterly fake people, and avoid engaging in debate with them. They will tire and bore you to death with statements that don't respond to the issue at hand, merely to boost their own image.

When we feel judged by a lot of people, we hide our true selves and try to look good. This is why virtue signalling is such a pervasive reality in today's social media. It's just noise on the internet and, like trolls, must be ignored. We must debate issues by saying things as they are, for only then can solutions be found.

Official India Hates Fun

We need to think consequences and global standards before we ban something outright

For some reason, Indians are officially supposed to hate fun. Small wonder then that our politicians or courts don't spare a moment to reconsider a decision that will kill someone else's enjoyment. As long as the intention is good, we don't mind crushing anything that is good fun, even though the decision might not really achieve anything worthwhile.

In our country, one of the biggest casualties of this mentality is alcohol. We see it as a sinful form of self-indulgence. We believe that the state should regulate its sale and consumption as strictly as possible, even if it means banning it altogether or making bizarre rules that lead to 5-star hotels emptying their minibars overnight.

The recent Supreme Court order prohibiting the sale of alcohol within 500 metres of a state highway is the latest such rule. Overnight, it has rendered thousands of businesses unviable, and has cost lakhs of people their jobs. This, when these businesses had invested huge sums of money, stupidly believing that (a) India is a country where rules cannot be changed overnight; (b) if you have the right licences, nobody can stop you from doing business; and (c) India is a good place to invest.

Of course, they may have been foolish to believe that the Indian government and legal system will protect businesses. Because while we may make ads about 'Make in India', once a businessman actually invests his money, the policy often changes to 'make life hell' for him.

However, the only apparent casualty so far seems to be people who sell and consume alcohol. And since they are seen as participating in a business that only creates 'pleasure' or 'fun', we seem to think it is morally okay to bash them. Of course, we are not interested in the damage it causes us.

One, it harms India's business-friendly image abroad. It shows foreign investors that we are a banana republic which changes rules on a weekly basis and that we cannot protect our investments. Two, it hits the economy of states which rely on tax revenues from alcohol to finance welfare sectors such as education and healthcare (yes, this sinful alcohol pays for many Indians' healthcare).

Three, it encourages an illicit liquor economy to crop up, because those who want alcohol will find a way to get it. Prohibition, or even restricted sales, has always failed worldwide. It only encourages bribes, corruption and under-the-counter alcohol-selling dhabas on the highway.

The funny part is, this 500 metre measure will not achieve its desired goal—to prevent people from drinking and driving on the state highways. If I have a vehicle, it will take me less than two minutes to take a 500 metre detour to get my fix of alcohol for the road. You really think this rule would deter anyone?

Another pointless add-on to the rule is there can be no signs pointing to liquor shops on the highway. Whoever thought of this idea has clearly never heard of Google Maps. Wherever you may happen to be, it will give you the location of every shop in the vicinity, not to mention helping you navigate the shortest route to get there.

Yes, drivers will soon have apps on their phones with signs that will say 'Refreshment Centre, wink, wink' all over the highway. They won't mention alcohol, but they will ensure you get to the right place.

Of course, the fact that state highways now pass through densely populated cities like Mumbai, and hundreds of establishments in malls and 5-star hotels had to close down for no reason, shows that the rule wasn't well drafted. It harms tourism, local economies, revenue collection and employment prospects on the one hand, and doesn't reduce the number of drunk drivers on the other. Pretty pointless, isn't it?

The only ways to keep drunk drivers off the road is by imposing heavy penalties and punishments on offenders, and to design an effective nationwide campaign highlighting the dangers of drunk driving. This is what is done all over the civilised world and there is no reason we shouldn't try the same approach.

Which brings us to the overall issue of the blanket bans and restrictions that India tends to announce every few weeks. Shouldn't we also consider, before we announce a draconian rule, the global standard? If India aspires to be one of the modern, developed and civilised nations of the world, can we adopt and adhere to some enlightened practices followed in other such countries? Alcohol sale is not restricted at all in many countries, and yet they have managed to reduce drunk driving to a large extent.

Rules of the 500 metre type only create chaos and damage the economy, while offenders can easily find ways to circumvent the new arbitrariness. Former US President Barack Obama used to meet people over a beer in the presence of the media. Achievers in every field, including CEOs of multinational companies, occasionally have a drink or two and still function pretty well. To judge alcohol only by its abusers seems pretty narrow-minded, at least so far as modern lifestyles and habits go. It is time India grew up and took notice of these changing attitudes and global standards.

Alcohol use should be moderate, of course, and drunk driving is a serious offence. While measures should exist to curb it, they should be sensible and directed towards solving the problem. In short, laws should not be arbitrary and pointless, and drafted so hastily that people might suspect the lawmakers themselves were under the influence.

@chetan_bhagat

You can't ban your way to a better society. Change is slow, and requires consensus, empathy towards the other side, education and love.

261 replies/ 564 retweets/ 4,363 likes

@chetan_bhagat

The Sikh police officer who saved the Muslim man. I don't care who's in power or what is your politics. That's the India I want and ever will want. Even if I am the only one left wanting it.

996 replies/ 1,634 retweets/ 11,340 likes

Fifty Shades of Intolerance

*Too bad if you don't like something; you can't let go
of civil behaviour*

One of the most misunderstood, out of control and
inconclusive debates we have had in recent times in
India is on tolerance. A section of people are concerned,
and many have returned awards and made statements in
the media, citing specific incidents including the Dadri
killing and the Kalburgi murder. Others feel India is a
tolerant place.

The fact remains that we can freely discuss rising
intolerance, or even attack the government for it. That a
billion-plus people with tremendous differences in culture
go about their daily lives in the same country shows that
we are, in fact, a tolerant nation.

Yet, people on both sides of the debate make their
point vehemently and are unwilling to listen to the other
side. This alone is a kind of intolerance.

The question remains. Is India tolerant or intolerant?
Can we be tolerant enough to say both the statements
are true at the same time?

The confusion comes from the question itself. There
is no one kind of tolerance. There can be religious
intolerance, caste intolerance, intolerance of economic
inequality, the internet trolls' variety of intolerance,

political intolerance, traffic intolerance, and intolerance of alternate opinions.

The fact that we blare horns in traffic shows clearly who we are as a society (all developed and most other Asian countries don't have horn-blarers on their roads). If you have a Twitter account, then the crude, insensitive comments that rule Twitter clearly suggest we are unwilling to treat differing opinions with dignity.

At the same time, it is unfair to suggest we are all intolerant.

Many Indians do not blare horns (a few idiots are enough to make the roads intolerably noisy). Most people on Twitter have a positive attitude. The same goes for religious intolerance. Most Indians may not believe in every religion, but they are happy to co-exist with people of other faiths.

Should we label such a society 'intolerant'? Should we blindly defend it as tolerant, despite being aware of the unpleasant things that are happening in our country? Or should we simply call it a real society where all shades exist, one that could work on being better? It is funny how neither side in the debate wants to come to a real conclusion.

How do we make India more tolerant? To answer this, it is important to understand the psychology of tolerance and keep it as independent of politics as possible. The dictionary defines tolerance as 'the ability or willingness to tolerate the existence of opinions or behaviour that one dislikes or disagrees with'.

Tolerance or intolerance in a society unfolds in a three-step process. One, there are things that bother us. Two, we choose to react to these bothersome things in specific ways. Three, these reactions can create certain perceptions and fears in society.

The first step, what bothers us, is most important. It's also the hardest to fix. We don't have to become a society where nothing bothers us. Bad roads, corruption, inefficiency, mediocrity and poverty should bother us. However, in these areas, we seem to be quite tolerant. We often elect corrupt or inept leaders.

What shouldn't bother you are people whose belief systems are different from yours—those who don't believe in your religion, culture, politics, and so on. You don't have to love them. However, you have to learn to live and let live. If our differences didn't bother us so much in the first place, intolerance would be nipped in the bud.

The only way this can happen, however, is through a long process of educating and exposing society to the various belief systems and cultures of the world. While that is happening in India with increased media exposure and migration of people, change will be slow.

This is why the second step, how we react to what bothers us, becomes important. Do we scream? Do we hit someone who doesn't agree with us? Do we abuse those who are different? Or can we control our emotions? Can we learn to take a deep breath and say, I don't like what the other person is saying or doing at all, but I will not react in a violent or uncivil manner?

It seems that many Indians have a hard time doing that. Here, it is almost culturally acceptable to be ill-mannered when you are upset. This needs to change. Too bad if you don't like something, you simply can't let go of civil behaviour.

The last step is illustrated by what violent or abusive reactions stemming from intolerance can do to society. For one, they create massive amounts of fear. A single incident of communal conflict or violence will create fear in the minds of millions of others. Add to that the over-eager and ever-present media of today, and fear spreads faster than ever before.

It is here that the top leadership can play a role. While the government doesn't need to comment on everything that happens, if an incident has the potential to frighten millions and make them insecure, it needs to be addressed at the top. And fast.

Ultimately, we hope to reach a day where Indians get bothered for the right reasons. Until then, we simply need to be well-mannered in our reactions. Those in power as well as the media should ensure that ill-conceived actions don't create fear in the minds of the people. We are a mixed society, tolerant and intolerant at the same time. Let us be tolerant enough to accept that for now and strive to make things better.

Will You Spend ₹80 to See India Win a Dozen Olympic Golds?

A professionally managed Olympics fund, supported by the Indian public, will guarantee at least a dozen golds for India at the next event

Every four years, a nation of over a billion people struggles to win medals at the Olympics. Some unfairly lash out at the sportspersons on social media. Other self-righteous types talk about how we should encourage them, how participation counts for something, and how that is what finally matters. Frankly, none of this is relevant to the country's sports scene. Nor will it help us win medals. So what will it take for India to win not just a bronze and a silver but a dozen golds, even three dozen medals in all (yes, it is possible!) at the Olympics?

Let's start by looking at some of the reasons commonly cited for our poor performance (and why they don't make sense). These are: one, we don't have money for sports (we actually don't need to spend that much on a per capita basis to make a difference); two, we don't have good sporting genes (a bizarre argument, as Indians are a very large and diverse gene pool); and three, parents don't encourage their kids to play sports in this country because it has no future as a career choice (partly true, but the same is the case abroad; for instance, silver-medallist rowers can't really have a lavish future awaiting them anywhere in the world).

In reality, there are three main reasons why we suck at the Olympics...

We just don't care much about Olympic sports (except when the Olympics is on and that is the cool thing to do).

We don't really value excellence in any field. Jugaad and mediocrity often work just fine, though they can't get us medals.

We don't spend enough on sports, or rather, channel funds in the right direction.

The first two are societal attitudes and values. They will change slowly, over time. The third, *how* we spend on sports, is the focus here. We have to understand the difference between spending on competitive sports and on sports in general. Sports is not all competition; it is also for recreation and exercise, which is important. For instance, we need to have more jogging tracks in our parks. These may not yield world-class athletes, but they will certainly raise the level of fitness in the neighbourhood. On the other hand, it also costs a lot to train athletes to win medals in competitive sports on the world stage. What should we do? There is no easy answer. You need a bit of both.

The need of the hour, however, is to end this humiliation. If India wins a dozen golds at the Olympics, there will be huge benefits. It will finally put the country on the sports map. It will motivate millions of youth to pursue excellence. It will invoke a stronger sense of national identity in us. This is one way of making India glorious, as political leaders like Narendra Modi aspire to do.

It is important at this stage to look at some numbers. Australia, with a population of just 20 million, averages around 50 medals in every Olympics. The total amount the country spends on sports is around ₹700 crore, of which 80 per cent (₹560 crore) goes into Olympic sports. India, on the other hand, has averaged around two medals per Olympics over the last two decades. The amount we spend? Well, the carve-out for sports in the Youth Affairs and Sports ministry budget is about ₹900 crore. Of this, over two-thirds goes into organising local-level tournaments (not likely to yield Olympic winners), prize money, upgrading stadiums, and schemes to uplift the Northeast.

This means only around ₹300 crore is available for actually improving the standard of sports in the country. And it isn't clear how much of that is invested in Olympic-level training. The talent search budget for the entire nation, for instance, is a mere ₹5 crore. Either way, even at a grossly overestimated ₹300 crore, the amount allocated on a per sport basis for the twenty-odd Olympic sports is only ₹15 crore. So we have a national budget of ₹15 crore for, say, swimming—a sport which could bring us a ton of medals. That probably just pays for the salaries of babus associated with the sport. Hence, the amount left over, to find and train new talent with, is nothing. Good luck making Olympic champions with that!

Australia, on the other hand, spends a far smaller amount in total on sports, but has lower overheads, less corruption, and absolute clarity about its goal—excellence in the Olympics.

India can do the same. For one, we need a separate budget—call it, say, the Indian Olympics Fund—for talent scouting and training for the event, apart from funds for promoting sports in general. This budget should be at least ₹10,000 crore per year. It may sound like a lot, but only amounts to ₹80 per Indian on a per capita basis.

Something like Nandan Nilekani's Aadhaar proposal, where the Olympics fund is entirely managed by external professionals, would keep things more honest and efficient. The money would be spent in three parts: one, to identify and maintain a talent pool of around 5,000 elite sportspersons (called Elite5000) in the country, preferably in medal-heavy events (such as swimming and cycling); two, on Elite5000 scholarships which will ensure an allowance for the education of these athletes so they don't have to worry about money or jobs later; and three, to give world-class training to Elite5000, of which around 300 will make up the Indian contingent at the Olympics. Such a setup will certainly win us a dozen golds at each event.

Medals do not just come from a fighting spirit fired by patriotic emotion, nor even from cheering our players on social media or turning individual sporting heroes into media stars. These things help, but they are and should be a given. Medals will come if we set up an Indian Olympics Fund along the lines suggested above. Now tell me, are you ready to pay ₹80 per year and feel the pride of India winning a dozen gold medals at every Olympics?

POLITICS, INDIA-STYLE

Over the last ten years, we've tried various types of governments. Tired of the last scam-ridden government, people finally voted in a majority government in 2014. What has that meant for us? And, as we go into another general election, what should we, as individuals, be looking at?

The Modi government has been criticised for cultivating an atmosphere that has stoked communalism. 'We are All Anti-nationals' talks about why we need to move beyond our religious affiliations. The section also includes essays that look at what the BJP needs to do to win elections; on why the party's self-goals are more dangerous than Rahul; how they can get their poll maths right; and the lessons they and the Congress can learn from the 2017 Gujarat elections. 'In These San-sad Times, Call a Virtual Session of Parliament' suggests ways by which politicians can be made more responsible, and how the functioning of Parliament can be improved. The damaging culture of 'favours' is addressed in 'Netas, Do Us a Favour: Don't Swap Favours'. Considering the RSS's influence over the government, ways in which they should change and thereby play a greater role in our society are brought up in 'Shorts First, Soul Next?'.

As is the rest of the world, India is also currently faced with crises related to terrorism and refugees seeking asylum. 'Rohingya Are Human, Too' talks about how—despite the accusations of their links with terrorist organisations—India needs to be more humane; we can tackle the problem without endangering ourselves and lift our image as a serious power and problem-solver in the region. 'Terrorism and Extremitis' asks that we stop getting polarised over the question of terrorism. It is not a right-wing or a left-wing issue, but one that affects us all.

Our relations with Pakistan are addressed in 'Uri Changed One Thing' and the essay explains why it does more damage than good to compare ourselves with them. 'The Parable of PK' talks about the need for out-of-box solutions, despite the international community's resistance to this.

Finally, 'What the Shattered AAP Dream Tells Us about Ourselves' talks about holding our governments accountable, despite all the disappointments.

The Rohingya Are Human, Too:
How We Can Deal with Refugees and Still Keep India Safe

By handling the Rohingya crisis both humanely and practically, India stands to strengthen its political presence in the South Asian region

News reports informed us that the BSF used pepper spray and stun grenades to stop Rohingya refugees from entering Indian territory. The government also seems keen to get rid of the Rohingya already in the country (their numbers are estimated at around 40,000), citing security threats.

Many of our TV news channels seem to agree. We have even heard news anchors screaming, 'Let the Rohingya be found floating around in the Indian Ocean. Don't dump them here.' Well, we are talking about human beings here. That includes children, women and elderly people. Some of these are people living in our own neighbourhoods today.

There are border villages of Myanmar's Rakhine province (where the Rohingya come from) which are not far (in the range of a hundred kilometres) from some towns in Mizoram. Ethnically, these people are Indo-Aryan. Their own country has marginalised them for decades. They are denied citizenship and passports, need state permission to marry (which takes years) and to travel to neighbouring villages, and are excluded from government jobs.

Worse, there is a systematic campaign of racism and hate against them in Myanmar. Imagine living in your own country like a hated outsider, denied basic rights, and watching people from your community getting routinely killed just for being who you are.

If you can understand this suffering as a human being, then it is perhaps also time to disclose that the majority of the Rohingya are Muslims. Does it make a difference? Is their suffering any less because of their religion?

So why are we pepper-spraying their kids and screaming to get them out?

There are several reasons. Some are actually valid. Others simply reek of our bigotry and lack of human empathy. They also ignore the potential benefits and opportunities that India gains by being a regional Big Brother.

But first, let's go over the valid reasons for not welcoming the Rohingya. According to the Indian government, some Rohingya in India may have terror links, or are at risk of radicalisation. This assessment is not inaccurate. Unfortunately, there are groups with fundamentalist leanings among the Rohingya.

To fight the injustice the Rohingya have been subjected to, organisations like the Arakan Rohingya Salvation Army (ARSA) have popped up. They use violent means to grab attention for their cause. In fact, the recent purge of the Rohingya by the Myanmar government was a result of ARSA terror attacks.

Hence, the Rohingya are not just seen as victims, but also as a community with significant radical elements. People who live in strife, have limited means, and are discriminated against, are more vulnerable to being indoctrinated. In fact, plenty of Indians fit these criteria and can be exploited in the same way.

Having said that, if we had a proper registry of the Rohingya in India, enabling us to monitor the community more closely, such probability is reduced. If we gave them legal refugee status in the country (rather than forcing them to hide from authorities) by issuing refugee cards, for instance, we could have a better idea of what they are up to. As in any community with radical elements, we would find that over 99 per cent of them are not terrorists.

Spraying them with pepper, or sending them back to the country that will probably kill them, doesn't seem like something a civilised, democratic and humane country would do. One of the reasons cited for doing so is the 'burden' refugees place on the state that hosts them. The fact that there are about a million Rohingya left in Myanmar is a matter of concern.

Most of these refugees move to Bangladesh, as most Rohingya territories in Myanmar border this country. In the recent exodus alone, Bangladesh received over 4,00,000 refugees, ten times as many as the total number of Rohingya who have sought refuge in India. These refugees fend for themselves, get very few state benefits and work mostly as daily wage labourers. Are they really going to create such a burden?

The bigger question is: how do we handle refugees in general? What would we have done, for example, if Hindus were persecuted in Pakistan to the point that they were all forced to run to us? Would we accept them and give them asylum, or would we pepper-spray them back?

We need to provide a mechanism for refugees from our neighbouring countries through which they can legally apply for asylum. If they can prove persecution—religious, ethnic or otherwise—they may be considered eligible. Economic reasons alone will not be enough to justify immigration. Once inside the country, these refugees would also be tracked by the state. They would be more obligated to inform the government of their movements and activities than regular citizens.

Of course, having a formal refugee policy doesn't mean India alone takes in refugees while the rest of the continent does nothing. Just as in the EU, there should be sharing arrangements in the ASEAN region to handle refugee crises. Richer nations can contribute more money towards the resettlement of asylum seekers.

Meanwhile, if India took the lead in handling the Rohingya crisis, it would lift our image as a serious power and problem-solver in the region. If we indulge in fearmongering and pepper-spraying instead, it will only show how immature we are.

Ultimately, the Myanmar government cannot be absolved of its actions which have created the crisis. To deny citizenship to people who have lived in your country for decades is deplorable and unjustifiable, whatever the rationale. Myanmar is a country with a Buddhist majority. We see Buddhism as one of the world's most non-violent religions. Hence, the extreme violence meted out to Rohingya is, frankly, shocking to most Indians.

India can play a big role in pressuring Myanmar to fix this problem peacefully. But we have to decide. Are we going to be the scared, xenophobic and close-minded India of the past, or a more open, humane and mature society?

How we treat the helpless at our door goes a long way in determining that.

Shorts First, Soul Next?

RSS should use all its influence with the government to push for 10 per cent growth, not Hindu culture

Something dramatic happened: the ninety-year-old Rashtriya Swayamsevak Sangh changed its uniform. The ubiquitous RSS khaki shorts will make way for brown trousers.

This change is superficial at one level. After all, a rose is a rose by any other name and an RSS worker is an RSS worker no matter what they wear. But it also shows the RSS intent to change with the times. In fact, the RSS today has a golden opportunity to contribute to India's progress, which is its stated mission. This can only happen if the organisation modifies its current ideology as well as some of the means it adopts to achieve its goals.

The RSS began life during the British Raj, as an organisation dedicated to bringing the Hindus of the country together to protect their interests. It was banned first during British rule and thrice after Independence—in 1948, when Nathuram Godse assassinated Mahatma Gandhi; then during the Emergency (1975–77); and after the demolition of the Babri Masjid in 1992. Some of these bans were political (the Congress saw the RSS as an adversary). Eventually, all of them were revoked.

Such a history does create trust issues for outsiders who wonder what this organisation is really about.

The official RSS website sums up its mission: 'Expressed in the simplest terms, the ideal of the Sangh is to carry the nation to the pinnacle of glory through organising the entire society and ensuring the protection of Hindu Dharma.' Further, 'Our one supreme goal is to bring to life the all-round glory and greatness of our Hindu Rashtra [...] Bharat must stand before the world as a self-confident, resurgent and mighty nation.'

The mission thus appears to be twofold: one, to restore India's glory in the world; and two, to organise and protect Hindu religion and culture. There is nothing wrong with these goals as such. Problems arise when the RSS uses certain methods to carry out this so-called mission.

Not all its actions are harmful. The RSS does some good charitable work. Its volunteers have helped out in almost all of India's recent natural disasters. Individual shakhas organise community work like morning fitness classes, helping millions across the nation.

However, problems arise from the RSS belief that nationalism must be inculcated in people even at the cost of personal liberties, from the imposition of RSS ideas about traditional Hindu culture being the essence of India's glory as well as the cornerstone of a peaceful and prosperous society. The two separate objectives of making India glorious again and protecting traditional Hindu culture are frequently intertwined for the RSS, which assumes one cannot happen without the other.

This is not true. Worse, this will not achieve the RSS objectives of building a glorious India and saving Hindu culture. So what will make India glorious? The first necessary (but not sufficient) condition for a country to be respected among the nations of the world is a certain level of prosperity, including higher per capita income and standards of living. We ourselves look up to countries richer than us. So if RSS wants a great India, it needs to focus on something it hasn't focussed on so far—the economy.

The RSS has tremendous influence over the government, and so far it has used this only to promote Hindu culture and a few charity initiatives. Instead, RSS should set up its own team of economists and demand 10 per cent GDP growth. When that is achieved, India will become rich, its youth will get jobs, people will be happier, and India will be respected. If you don't have money in your pocket, the world is not going to listen to you.

The second condition for a glorious country is a free society, where citizens have the liberty to make life choices—which god to pray to and how much, who to love and how much, how patriotic one needs to be and how to express that patriotism. The moment you get into imposition mode, some of that glory and greatness is lost.

North Korea makes its citizens chant slogans about its greatness on a regular basis. Does anyone take that nation seriously? It is in free societies that people, ideas, culture and art thrive, creating a huge impact on the world. If you take away people's liberties to restore order, you won't get glory. You will only get a fascist reputation.

As for helping Hinduism prosper, it will help if the RSS becomes more inclusive by reaching out to Dalits, women and Muslims. These sections of our society need to be represented on RSS high-level committees and boards. All RSS heads in the past have been upper-caste Hindus. Membership is almost entirely Hindu. Is this spreading Hindu culture or building a cult?

If RSS implements these changes, it can play a far greater role in Indian society and go a long way towards achieving its objectives. While the RSS is affiliated to the BJP, it doesn't face similar political pressures. It can take on some issues that the BJP can't address. Its statement about reservation policies needing to be reviewed, for instance, was welcome, for no political party in India has the courage to say this. It may have cost the BJP government the Bihar elections, but should the RSS be more concerned about the Bihar polls than restoring India's glory? Nation first, politics later. Never dilute that.

Greater emphasis on the economy, inclusiveness, and putting the nation first, will be a shift in focus that both the RSS and India as a whole could benefit from. It is not only the shorts, but also the soul of the organisation, that needs a bit of a change. Hope we see that change soon.

We Are All Anti-nationals: The Equation D+M>H Explains Indian Politics, but D+M+H Is a Better Combo

We need to move beyond divisive vote bank politics and sectarian identities to build a better India

Whoa, what's happening? It used to be BJP versus the rest, the tolerant fighting pitched battles with the intolerant. How and when did it become nationalists versus anti-nationals?

A couple of kids protested at JNU. No big deal there, as that campus probably has more protests than classroom lectures. However, this article is not a judgement on JNU, though it is about time that university began to behave like one.

This article aims to examine the labelling of people as 'anti-India' or 'anti-national' and why there is so much of that going around. From award wapsi to the JNU protests, someone is always being asked to go to Pakistan. In asking why, this article will not take sides. When both sides behave stupidly, it is best just to watch.

So, what is going on? Essentially, Indian politics is governed by the equation: D+M>H.

Sorry to be nerdy, but let me explain. D refers to Dalits, or rather all lower caste voters (including SCs, STs, BCs and OBCs). You could call it the Downtrodden vote. M refers to the Muslim vote. Again, if you prefer political correctness, you could call it the Minority vote. H refers to the upper caste Hindu vote. The greater-than symbol means that the Downtrodden plus Minority vote is always greater than the upper caste Hindu vote.

Let's say that D is roughly 40 per cent, M is 20 per cent, and H accounts for 40 per cent of the vote bank. Of course, these numbers are vastly oversimplified. But they help understand the political dynamic in our country today.

This equation means that, under normal circumstances, the BJP can almost never be the ruling party. It isn't surprising that in the nearly seventy years that have elapsed since Independence, BJP has been in power for less than seven.

The only way BJP can form a government is when one or more of the following happen. One, the D+M vote gets divided due to multiple parties competing for the same vote. Two, D and M separate from each other in a particular election. Three, the BJP projects a charismatic candidate who woos some D and even a few M votes to the H side.

In the 2014 Lok Sabha elections, all this happened, propelling Modi to victory. In the recent Bihar election, parties opposing the BJP ensured D+M did not split, and they won. In Delhi, in 2015, AAP not only got the D+M vote but also managed to slice out a fair chunk of H.

Why does D+M vote in constant opposition to H? Well, D and M both feel persecuted by upper class Hindus who they feel have denied them opportunities. D+M is such a sizeable chunk of the vote that many political parties woo them. They feed the victimisation theory in order to do so.

The eventual solution for uplifting D and M lies in their focussing on educating and modernising themselves. Since that is difficult, the political parties representing them often resort to agendas that attack H, and H's aspirations.

The Congress has always enjoyed the D and M vote. SP, BSP, TMC, RJD and JD(U) are other parties who seek this vote. Even AAP realises the value of this vote, hence its constant attacks on Modi.

Meanwhile, the H vote sees things differently. It doesn't feel like a victim; hence, there is no inherent need for retribution. In fact, H can even dream of a better India. It aspires to build a nation that is prosperous, free and respected in the world. Since D+M wants to annoy H, it often enjoys seeing these H aspirations being punctured.

This is where the 'anti-national' narrative is born. H wonders why D+M, already appeased by reservations, does not move along and share its aspirations. Aren't they anti-national in refusing to dream big, like itself? Meanwhile, D+M thinks: how dare H dream big while we are suffering? India owes us first. How dare H impose its national aspirations on us?

This fundamental tussle is what generates our daily politics. Sadly, it also allows true anti-nationals to divide us. A terrorist group infiltrates and attacks India. Parties which seek the D+M vote, afraid of upsetting them, do not condemn it enough. Similarly, a fringe H group makes an outrageous Hindutva statement. The BJP doesn't condemn it enough, so as not to antagonise the H vote.

In this constant D-M-H conflict there is one casualty—India. But the equation doesn't have to be this way. D+M+H is a better combo, and it can decide who to vote for based on real issues rather than merely to settle scores.

The politicians like this divide. It allows them to be relevant just by feeding the conflict, rather than focussing on real work. And we citizens can't seem to get past it either. But if we don't all come together as a nation, aren't we all anti-nationals?

D has to integrate and engage with H, and come up with a better plan than perennial reservations which only maintains the divide. M has to realise that India comes first, religion later. H has to stop imposing its culture and views on others, and understand not everyone thinks the way they do.

We need to come together, listen to all sides and resolve our differences. Work on moving beyond our D, M or H affiliations. Until only 'I' remains, which stands for India. And that is when we will no longer deserve the 'anti-national' label.

@chetan_bhagat

If there are people here who can think beyond whether it was the BJP or Congress' fault and think about what is actually good for the country, let me know. Would be nice to see some people who actually care about India first.

532 replies/ 335 retweets/ 3,550 likes

@chetan_bhagat

The Modi wave even at its peak gave BJP a few %age points vote share lead. With the wave ebbing, and opposition uniting, simple arithmetic making it very difficult for the BJP to win in several places. Good or bad, shows what 2019 could be like for India.

243 replies/ 164 retweets/ 1,261 likes

To Get Poll Maths Right, BJP Needs to Remember Three Numbers

Catering to different kinds of voters is the only way the BJP can win against a united Opposition in 2019

By the time you read this, dozens of articles will have appeared on what the BJP did wrong in Bihar. Prescriptions on what the BJP should do now have also been given—from reining in Hindutva elements to speeding up reforms. The party, meanwhile, has cited the official reason for the defeat as 'getting the voter arithmetic wrong'. If it was indeed about the arithmetic, then the BJP could solve its problems by simply buying a few nice Vedic math calculators. It is arithmetic and more.

In the previous Bihar assembly election of 2010, the BJP–JDU combine secured 39 per cent of the votes. Opponents RJD and Congress competed separately, but still garnered 35 per cent. Seems pretty close, right? However, the BJP + JDU alliance won a staggering 205 out of the 243 seats in 2010 despite a vote share that was just five points higher than their competitors'. This was because the opponents of the BJP + JDU had competed against each other and their votes did not add up. But this time, the JDU + RJD + Congress combo landed 42 per cent of the votes and won 178 seats. The BJP and its allies got 34 per cent, and won only 58 seats. Again, an eight-point vote share difference led to a landslide defeat for the BJP.

So, does the official BJP line of 'just bad arithmetic' make sense? Not really. The BJP needs to remember only three numbers (in terms of percentage) if it wants to win elections: 25, 33 and 40.

25 per cent is the BJP's cult vote share or the bhakt vote share. No matter what happens, even in the worst of times, the BJP seems to garner this percentage of the votes. In Bihar 2015, despite the drubbing, it had a vote share of 24.4 per cent. In Lok Sabha 2009, when UPA II won big, BJP still had a 25 per cent vote share. This is no mean feat. A cult following in at least a quarter of the electorate is something to be valued and preserved. However, this 25 per cent also consists of all the Muslim-hating, Pakistan-hating, homosexual-hating, feminism-hating, anybody-who-is-not-like-us-hating voters. These are voters who love Hindu supremacy and want beef banned. This core support is what the BJP doesn't want to lose at any cost, for it defines them and keeps them credible in the worst of times.

However, here's some news for the BJP people who seem to have got their arithmetic wrong—this 25 per cent is not enough.

I won't go into value judgements on how the values held by some of these voters are regressive, bigoted and wrong for India. Few listen to moral arguments in politics. It's not about morals, it's about the math. Luckily for

India, and unfortunately for the BJP, this 25 per cent cult is not enough to win elections. Also, this vote bank is maintained at a cost. It is because of them that Muslims, comprising 15–20 per cent of the electorate, do not vote for the BJP. The media doesn't like this 25 per cent either, which in turn makes them hostile to the BJP whenever the latter panders to them. With the media being so powerful today, preserving this 25 per cent means upsetting the remaining 75 per cent of the electorate.

Hence, to win, provided the BJP's opponents do not gang up against them, the vote share they need to secure is the second number—33 per cent, 8 points more than the core 25 per cent. This is what the BJP had in the Lok Sabha elections of 2014, when the Opposition was disorganised, and this share helped them win big. However, the party had to work hard for this extra 8 per cent. It involved taking on a development-oriented agenda, engaging with industry, building support among the youth, working on the OBC vote bank, and projecting Modi as a capable leader while making some rather lofty promises. This 8 per cent non-bhakt vote came from fence-sitters who voted for reform and believed for once that the BJP would deliver it. Though small in size, this set of voters was crucial. It was also not unconditional in its love. Unfortunately, the BJP did not continue to nurture them after the election.

40 per cent is what the BJP needs to win when its opponents gang up, like they did in Bihar. That alliance is why, despite garnering 34 per cent of the vote, the party

lost badly. Securing this 40 per cent is a scary scenario for the BJP. To pull this off, it not only needs to keep its cult base, but also fulfil the promises made to the non-bhakt 8 per cent and then win a further 7 per cent vote share from people sceptical of the BJP. One would have expected the BJP to demonstrate this with its exemplary performance after 2014. As the results show, it didn't. If the Opposition gangs up again like it did in Bihar, it will be very tough going for the BJP in Lok Sabha 2019.

This is all the maths the BJP needs to remember—25, 33, 40. It needs to take a risk with its cult, and do something to please the crucial 8 per cent for now. Big bang reforms, real action against specific people who spread communal intolerance, and sensitivity on OBC issues will help. Lower taxes will too, as much of the 8 per cent consists of taxpayers.

Keep every percentage point of your vote share happy to stay in power, and build on that. Cults don't win elections. Political parties which are inclusive and capable of pleasing different kinds of voters do. It is time the BJP understood this. Or it will fail the maths test again.

In these San-sad Times, Call a Virtual Session of Parliament

The ruling party, the Opposition and citizens must act together to ensure sessions of Parliament are not wasted

I don't know what is more disturbing: the fact that entire sessions of Parliament are routinely washed out in our country, or that we aren't as bothered by this fact as we should be. What can we do about it anyway? We didn't like the previous government, under which Parliament had ceased to work. So we elected a new majority government. Now even this government can't seem to make Parliament work. What are we to do?

Take Parliament's monsoon session in 2015, for instance. Some blame the Congress: they disrupted proceedings, so it is their fault. Others point fingers at the BJP for shielding its ministers. Proving our opponents' party wrong seems to preoccupy us more than the fact that an entire session of Parliament was wasted.

We should be worried. If India just needed to maintain status quo in its policies and laws, the disruption would have mattered less. However, India is nowhere near the nothing-needs-to-change stage. We haven't had a strong round of fundamental economic reforms since 1991. We don't have a 10 per cent GDP growth rate, which we need to fulfil the aspirations of millions of young people. Doing business in India is still extraordinarily difficult; until that situation improves, a spurt in job growth won't happen.

What can we do? Well, the BJP, the Congress and all of us citizens need to change a few things if we don't want to be stuck in this deadlocked democracy forever.

First, it is in the best interests of the party in power, the BJP, to make Parliament work. This government still doesn't have a corrupt image, despite the current controversies. However, what it doesn't need is an image of ineffectiveness—of a government that can't manage the country's affairs or work with others in order to do so. What could it have done differently, for instance, in the case of Parliament's monsoon session in 2015? First, even before the session started, the BJP could have addressed the issues related to Sushma Swaraj, Vasundhara Raje and Shivraj Singh Chouhan better. It chose to remain silent. Yes, these controversies were not comparable to the CWG or 2G scams. However, there were infractions and errors of judgement in Lalit Modi's case.

A simple way to test this is to ask: would the government do it again? If the answer is 'no', then a clarification at least would be in order, if not a resignation. In the Vyapam case, for example, there was a need to ensure a fair inquiry. If the BJP had accepted this fast, it could have come across as humble, receptive and responsive. More importantly, it could have played the controversy on its own terms and defused the Congress attack. By then it was too late, however, and the party acted after being pushed into a corner. Eventually, they had to relent and offer multiple explanations, including Swaraj's, in Parliament. The BJP really needs to learn to play on the front foot, even when it has made mistakes. Moreover, it needs to go easy on the Gandhi family bashing. They have lost that game already, and the jokes are old.

The Congress is also at fault. In politics, the opponent's weaknesses are fair game. Of course, when the ruling party is embroiled in controversies, it is a tantalising opportunity to attack. But the party tends to punch far above its 44-member strength. There is only so much politics one should play. The Congress should do the right thing during sessions of Parliament and let the essential bills pass. Sure, attack your political opponent, but don't harm the country.

Finally, we citizens are also to blame. We are easily fooled into the 'Congress did it' or 'BJP did it' narrative. We forget that we are one country. There are no BJP bills or Congress bills, only good-for-India bills or bad-for-India bills. We should chide the BJP for not coming clean on controversies earlier, and also the Congress for placing politics above work. This constant taking of sides—'my politician is always right, the opponent always wrong—' is highly detrimental to democratic processes. Whether on Twitter or in Parliament, polarisation will get us nowhere. Instead, let us look at innovative ways to prevent washout sessions. Here are two suggestions.

First, let us demand a common agenda across political parties. Once that is hammered out, seeing it through should become a priority for Parliament. When common agenda items are under discussion, no disruptions should be allowed at all.

Second, it is about time we gave up some of the outdated, colonial formalities of Parliament and embraced technology. MPs can raise their hand to vote on bills, but if needed they can also vote using secure logins on their personal devices. Comments can be posted on Speaker-moderated virtual parliament groups. Citizens can view these comments, and judge the productivity of the sessions as well as the performance of their representatives. This will end the shouting matches and physical disruptions.

We don't always have to run Parliament virtually, but the option should be available if the Opposition is playing havoc to the extent that entire sessions are wasted. Let us come together, get our act together and take India forward.

Netas, Do Us a Favour: Don't Swap Favours

'Favour'-based friendships between politicians and businessmen are detrimental to the greater good

In the Hollywood classic *The Godfather*, the eponymous character, Don Corleone, runs a mafia family business. One of his key business strategies is granting favours to people. There is an understanding that the person taking the favour 'might' have to return it another day. It's a calculated move, yet the arrangement is pretty loose. The nature and timing of the return favour, and whether it will even be taken, is unknown. One of the Don's most famous lines in the film is: 'Someday—and that day may never come—I'll call upon you to do a service for me. But until that day, accept this justice as a gift on my daughter's wedding day.'

Powerful people work like that. They have a reserve of power, which they can use to help other powerful people and get help in return. It's an amazing system to multiply power. And if you know India well, you know that our high and mighty operate in exactly the same way.

Money and power mix well. Hence, alliances of industrialists and politicians (often called 'close family friendships') are common. In particular, businessmen in highly regulated sectors tend to network with politicians more closely than others.

On the surface, one can claim there is nothing wrong with it. After all, what is wrong in making friends and helping them? Sometimes this help might be extended by one of the partners when the other is in genuine distress. Also, since the nature and timing of a return favour—or whether one will ever be taken—is unknown, who can find fault in these exchanges?

Such behaviour becomes even harder to classify as right or wrong when the help is not monetary in nature, as in the case of a politician being paid heaps of money for passing a shady tender. That would be a straightforward bribe, a direct give-and-take transaction, something most Indians understand as corruption. Favours are much harder to classify.

What then is the issue? Why do people get so agitated when DLF gives Robert Vadra cheap land, or if some ministers help Lalit Modi? Maybe the owners of DLF did genuinely love Vadra, and wanted to give him a gift to kick-start his business. After all, they didn't ask for anything in return right then. Maybe the ministers are fond of Lalit Modi as a person and a friend, and all they want to do is help him out, while not technically breaking any laws. Isn't it okay then?

Well, it isn't. The problem arises because every time a politician (or his or her relative) accepts a big favour, a return favour is booked as due in their account. What the nature of that favour will be, and when it will be sought, is unknown. Similarly, whenever a politician grants a powerful person a big favour, it often means a favour was taken by the former before or will be taken later.

This business of exchanging favours with powerful businessmen is not what our politicians were elected for, in the first place. They were elected to do the country a favour. They are supposed to spend their time, energy and judgement, and use their power, for one purpose only—to take decisions in the best interests of the nation. When they trade favours with a chosen few, at some level, the nation is betrayed. Voters' trust is eroded when they find out their leader is busy collecting and granting favours, supposedly in the name of friendship, but only to a select few.

It is the politician who is mostly at fault here, because he or she is representing the people. However, it is unfair to only blame the political class for this favour-swapping culture. We Indians love to take favours from the powerful whenever we get the opportunity. From booking railway tickets to getting government jobs, we have little hesitation in asking someone in power to help us, even at the cost of compromising fairness and merit. Our business community is at fault too, as they jump at any chance to cosy up to politicians.

From 'harmless' Diwali gifts and invites to weddings and parties, to offering their business resources for political purposes including election funding, clever businessmen are keen to do politicians all kinds of favours, only to have them return these someday. Sadly, the return favour sought by a businessman from a politician is often unethical. In such circumstances, our netas need to be extra careful and avoid the temptation of taking favours. There is no such thing as a free lunch; no businessman ever did anything for a politician out of sheer love.

All of us need to rethink our boundaries in friendships and relationships when it comes to favours. Are we as a culture going to place the greater good above personal need or greed? Or do we want to operate like the mafia, helping ourselves and those close to us, even at the expense of the nation?

The best strategy is to try and avoid taking favours, as that's where the slippery slope begins for politicians. Bollywood is rarely the inspiration for what one should do in life, but one line from Salman Khan's *Bodyguard* is memorable. 'Do me a favour,' he says. 'Don't do me any favours.'

Would be nice if our politicians put this line up outside their offices, wouldn't it?

@chetan_bhagat

Expecting politics without unethical behaviour is like
expecting Jalebis without sugar and oil. Theoretically
possible, practically does not work. The best we can
hope for is nothing illegal. Ethics work on twitter,
not in hung houses.

561 replies/ 692 retweets/ 3,894 likes

@chetan_bhagat

Less bullets. More bullet trains. Keep rising India.

289 replies/ 749 retweets/ 6,049 likes

Terrorism and Extremitis

To stop terrorism, we must avoid stepping into polarisation traps set by the internet

Quick question. What do the following cities have in common: Brussels, Istanbul, Paris, Nice, Berlin, Orlando, London and Manchester. Well, apart from being prominent, affluent global cities, they have all been subject to major terror attacks linked to the Islamic State (IS).

These attacks have claimed hundreds of innocent lives. They have also created fear in the minds of millions of people. Cities like Paris and London are expected to be safe. If terrorists can carry out missions in the greatest First World cities, what hope remains for the rest of the world?

In fact, since June 2014, when ISIL proclaimed itself to be the Islamic State, it has 'conducted or inspired' over seventy terrorist attacks in twenty countries, a running total estimated by CNN. These figures do not include IS activities in its home base of Syria and Iraq, where thousands more have died in terrorist atrocities.

India has suffered from terrorism. So has Pakistan. And it turns out, the First World too is no longer immune.

There seems to be no solution in sight. In many countries, terrorism has become a political issue.

However, it tends to polarise and divide people rather than bringing them together to solve the problem.

In other words, the issue of terrorism today has become yet another casualty of extremitis, a disease endemic to the era of the internet. Today, on social media, it is difficult to be heard if you have a balanced, practical or nuanced approach to solving any problem. Things are either 'amazing' or a 'disaster'. Modi is either loved or hated. Trump is either '100 per cent right' or 'completely stupid'. You are either a 'patriot' or an 'anti-national'.

The argument that every situation might have pros and cons is considered a weak one. Truth and facts are irrelevant. Reason and logic don't matter. What matters above all are your feelings, and which side you are on. Say hello to extremitis, a nasty by-product of mass social conversations.

The same social media that was expected to open minds and expose people to various points of view, has now become the world's biggest polariser. The issue of terrorism is a case in point. Extremitis would have us believe that terrorism can only be one of two things. One, it is 'completely the fault of Islam', and hence 'Muslims should be banned'. On the other side of terrorism extremitis are the ultra-liberals. They believe that 'these terror attacks are not linked to a particular religion' and those claiming otherwise are 'Islamophobes' and 'racists'.

Thus, extremitis generates a lot of noise and juicy headlines. It doesn't really solve anything. Meanwhile, the IS's ever-expanding footprint covers new cities and countries, and perpetrates fresh atrocities.

We need to stop getting polarised over the question of terrorism. It is not a right-wing or a left-wing issue, but one that affects us all. And while terrorism doesn't have a religion, there's no denying that IS, the most active global terrorist organisation at large today, follows a radicalised version of Islam. Hiding or denying this truth in the name of political correctness doesn't help anyone either.

The (mis)use of Islam to recruit terrorists puts the onus on the Muslim community in general, and Islamic countries in particular, to play an active part in solving the problem. The fact that radical Islamic organisations are able to generate funds for their activities is one of the reasons terrorism has reached epic proportions in the world today. To counter them, other kinds of Islamic organisations need to be created and funded by governments around the world. These modern, moderate and liberal Muslim organisations need not have guns, but they need to be prominent and influential enough to stand up to their fundamentalist counterparts.

Also, Islam is the only religion which has spawned over a dozen theocracies or officially Islamic countries. Many of these are not democracies, and hence religious fundamentalists have a big say in how these countries are run. This complicates the problem, and is perhaps the reason why radical Islamic terror has thrived more than extremism motivated by other faiths. However, the rest of the world has to get together and put pressure on these countries, through diplomatic, economic or other means, to cultivate a zero tolerance policy on terrorism.

Holding fundamentalist beliefs may well fall within the parameters of religious choice. However, when innocent people get hurt, all bets are off.

Many of these Islamic countries have strict zero tolerance laws against narcotics, for instance, and are successful in keeping their countries drug-free. Similarly, they should be able to commit to zero tolerance for terrorism.

Back home in India, we have to do the same. Terrorism is a hard threat to counter. Only a zero tolerance approach works. Hence, our home-grown terror apologists (the types who say terrorists are 'just misguided youth') should be condemned.

A zero tolerance policy does not amount to asking for a 'Muslim ban' or labelling a religion as evil. At the same time, it doesn't pussyfoot around the issue in the name of political correctness either.

The solution to terrorism will not come from extreme points of view, but from taking a nuanced and practical middle stance based on logic and reason. It is time we took a break from extremitis, and worked together to make the world and our country a safer place.

Gujarat's Perfect Verdict: How Gujaratis Managed to Keep Both BJP and Congress on their Toes

The Gujarat election results in 2017 were a timely lesson in accountability and balance for both our major political parties

Gujarat saw a Goldilocks election in 2017. Meaning, the election results were 'just right'. BJP won for a whopping sixth time, after ruling the state for over two decades. To win a majority, despite the usual anti-incumbency that sets in after such a long spell in power, is a major feat.

The PM's appeal is still intact in his home state, despite radical and controversial policy decisions such as demonetisation and GST. It looks like, just as Sonia backs Rahul, Gujarat continues to back its son, Modi. The party's 2017 win in Himachal Pradesh, securing nearly two-thirds of the seats, was also cause for celebration for the BJP.

And yet, things didn't go exactly as BJP had anticipated. The margin of victory in Gujarat was not like their Uttar Pradesh triumph a few months earlier, where BJP captured 75 per cent of the seats. In Gujarat, BJP won 99 of 182 seats, or 54 per cent of the total. But the Congress won 77 seats which, though a losing figure, is not a washout.

Many had thought Gujarat would be the safest state for the BJP. No matter what they did, Gujaratis would continue to support the party because of, well, Modi. But 2017 was hardly a cakewalk for the BJP in the state. It won due to a combination of sheer luck, better booth-level management, Congress's lack of confidence, and Modi's political smarts outsmarting Rahul's.

In other words, it was a hard-fought and hard-won election that the Congress came pretty close to winning too. If a dozen assembly seats had gone the other way and the Congress had come to office, there would have been a tectonic shift in Indian politics. If Modi had lost Gujarat in 2017, the BJP's consequent loss of face and the corresponding boost in the Opposition's morale would have seriously impacted the run-up to the 2019 Lok Sabha polls.

No wonder that at one point in the vote-counting, when the Congress was ahead, the BSE Sensex dropped almost a thousand points. The stock market recouped the losses when BJP won, breathing a sigh of relief that the government was stable and Modi in control again. Hence, just this scare of a possible BJP defeat is reason enough for Congress to celebrate.

However, after the celebrations are done, it is time for both parties to reflect on what they are doing wrong. The canny Gujarati voter has rapped the BJP's knuckles without actually throwing it out. They have also encouraged the Congress, but love isn't overflowing in that direction either.

The BJP needs to realise that while, electorally, the Modi brand is a golden asset, he is not a god or a superhero. Yes, those comparisons might work well as a marketing ploy, but in reality Modi is someone who gives the party a solid edge in the polls. He boosts the BJP vote share by 5–10 per cent, depending on the state, the situation and the type of election. Normally, such swings are enough for a party to win. However, to take this for granted is a mistake.

Of late, the BJP is making the 'pure vikas' voter, the fence-sitters who transferred loyalties to the party in 2014, nervous. The ruling party's silence on love jihad murders and opportunism during the *Padmavati* controversy, their strategic muteness on hardline Hindutva in general, has been unsettling. The voters who finally began to trust the BJP in 2014 get nervous when the party panders to its hardliner base. This pandering was the reason why BJP seldom won in the past.

The Hindus like their religion, but they don't generally like impositions, bullying, and a general atmosphere in which one feels scared. Eventually, the right Opposition leader can harness this fear. For the BJP, the lesson is simple—more Vajpayee and less Advani, please.

As for the Congress, they need to realise there is still a lot of work to be done. Rahul isn't 'back', as some say, and their improved performance in Gujarat is not because of him. A lot of Congress gains came from the BJP's mistakes, which accumulated over twenty-two years of rule in the state, especially their mishandling of certain movements (like the Patidar agitation). A lot of sympathy and encouragement that Congress is getting these days on social media comes from people who are scared of the BJP and are desperately seeking political alternatives, whatever those might be.

This is not the same as people being attracted to Rahul or the Congress. Waiting for BJP self-goals is not a pro-active Opposition strategy, and is unlikely to yield quick results. The Congress has to set its own agenda. Moreover, rather than praising Rahul Gandhi for every trivial reason they can find, it is better to acknowledge that he still has a long way to go.

In terms of running a grassroots party as well as capitalising on political opportunities as Modi does, Rahul has a lot to learn. For instance, Modi milking Mani Shankar Aiyar's 'neech' comment to his own advantage is not something every politician can pull off. To hold the most powerful office in the country, and still be able to play a victim in the eyes of the public, is an art form. Rahul needs to learn it. Else, the Congress cannot hope to traverse the narrow margin of the Gujarat results or gain significant victories in other states.

However, the 2017 Gujarat election may have benefited India in the long run. It showed the BJP that they must tone down support to hardliners, and that there was a real opposition to reckon with. For the Congress, it was an incentive to work harder, showing them a way to power, though it may still be far.

The Gujaratis have spoken. We owe them thanks for having pushed both our national political parties to reflect and work harder.

@chetan_bhagat

There are some Modi haters who want me to write hate tweets about Modi govt else they threaten to keep calling me biased. Not going to work. Have roughly an equal no of articles pro-anti BJP/Cong. So I know what I am doing. Sorry I can't be a mouthpiece of your hate.

636 replies/ 1,140 retweets/ 6,396 likes

Self-goals a Bigger Threat to BJP than Rahul

The BJP must introspect and drop its hardliner stance on basic liberties to retain fence-sitter votes in the upcoming elections

Just before Rahul Gandhi took the stage to address Indians at an event in New York a few years ago, Sam Pitroda, a Gandhi family adviser-friend-loyalist of long standing, said, 'We don't need advice for Rahul Gandhi.'

There you go. An incoming Congress president doesn't need advice. In any case, he seems to be having a comeback moment. His recent tweets have trended and, unlike in the past, not for the wrong reasons. Rahul also managed some traction in Gujarat. While most believe a Congress win is unlikely, one major opinion poll predicted a neck-and-neck race. Fine, no advice wanted or needed here for the present, I guess.

But what about the BJP? Do they care about advice? Or don't they need it either, as they have Narendra Modi, the vote magnet? Can they entertain the thought that they might be doing some things wrong?

I hope they do. Because while a major BJP defeat may not be in the offing, seeds of a political upset are being sown right now. The BJP has not been immune to the hubris that often comes with power. Rahul's perceived incompetence has added to this complacency. Who else would Indians vote for anyway?

However, some shifts are visible. The number of 'Pappu' jokes have reduced. The media is not as dismissive of Rahul as it was before. What's happening?

In UPA II, the defining image of Sonia Gandhi and Suresh Kalmadi laughing over a private joke during the AICC convention, at the height of the CWG scam, sealed the fate of the Congress. It signalled that not only was the party mired in corruption, it just didn't care. We all know what happened next.

As for the BJP, their defining vice is not corruption, at least not at levels that can agitate the Indian public. The BJP's vices are what they have always been—its love of fundamentalism and use of authoritarianism against those who oppose this. For no matter how many Obamas its leaders meet or global investor conferences they host, the BJP can't help but expose these two ugly traits.

Despite quoting Moody's and the World Bank, the party's support for regressive Hindu voices is unsettling for the new BJP voters who boarded the Modi bandwagon in 2014 for the sake of development. While the BJP's support of these fringe voices is not overt, their silence on some recent events is unsettling. This, along with the tendency to browbeat opposing voices, creates unease in a number of Indians. Will this unease convert to a vote switch?

Here are two specific examples of government actions (or lack of action) in recent years that have created an atmosphere of unease that could hurt the BJP's chances in Lok Sabha 2019.

One, *Padmavati*. While it was just a song-and-dance movie, how the government handled this controversy might well have determined how the Modi regime will be judged in the upcoming elections. Legally, the filmmakers did nothing wrong. Historically, there was no evidence of a clear, existing narrative on Padmavati, who might even be a fictional character.

Which brings us to the only factor responsible for the furore around the film: the sentiments of a section of the hardliner vote bank. That too, before the film was even released. Sure, some people might find the song-and-dance treatment of a story about a culturally respected character offensive. You have every right to condemn the film, but to prevent its release and threaten the filmmakers is plain wrong. It amounts to muzzling freedom of expression. If the BJP supports a ban to pander to hardliners, it will not only be a black mark on Modi's legacy but will also add to voter unease.

The second example is the handling of a relatively weak story about Jay Shah gaining business advantages after the 2014 elections. Top BJP leaders defended Jay Shah, to the extent of obtaining gag orders against reporting on the issue. However, the actual defence against the allegation would have been quite a simple matter. Amit Shah had a fair amount of power even before 2014 when the BJP ruled Gujarat. Could he not have helped his son's business benefit then? This easy rebuttal would have been sufficient.

These are times where major media houses practise self-censorship, when it comes to reporting on malpractice at the top levels. Judicial overreach is at an all-time high as well. From forcing movie theatres and audiences to honour the national anthem, to preventing the media from reporting on important cases, corruption and unethical behaviour is all around us.

The government isn't directly responsible for all of this. However, people link rising authoritarianism in governance to the BJP. If Rahul is seen as more consensus-driven, less feared and more accommodating, he may attract not only media support but a significant section of voters too. These fence-sitter voters, as 2014 showed us, are crucial.

While Rahul may not be a substantial threat, the BJP might do well to introspect. It isn't always the strong opponent who defeats you. Sometimes, self-goals can do the trick just as well.

What the Shattered AAP Dream Tells Us about Ourselves

When a movement becomes a government, the only way to remain accountable is to not compromise on core values even at the cost of losing elections

A quick online check reveals that an economy class return ticket to London would cost ₹45,000. A business class ticket, which gets you flat beds, lounges and exotic wines, is worth around ₹2,00,000. However, even this mode of travel was not good enough for a certain AAP minister, going by news reports. He preferred to travel first class to London, which costs a whopping ₹4,00,000.

Of course, ministers don't pay for these tickets themselves. They charge it to the government. So, in effect, the taxpayer pays for it. The reasons for travel (there have been other trips to Brazil, Finland and other destinations) are often flimsy—random seminars, casual student body invites, anything at all that gets them out of the world's most polluted city, I guess.

And, of course, first class is just more comfortable. You get four more inches of seat width and ten more inches of legroom. Most important, the wine selection is better. And there's exclusivity. Even CEOs travel business class. First class is for billionaires, big movie stars and, of course, the great take-metro-to swearing-in-ceremony AAP.

This would all be really funny if it hadn't actually happened. This is a real party that literally arose from the streets. This is about real Indians who gave AAP their trust and hope. We stood up for corruption, threw out a scam-tainted government and backed a new party. A party we thought would respect and protect our faith in them. A party that claimed to embrace simplicity as a virtue. Remember how people quit Apple and Google to join the AAP? Have you heard of that happening anywhere else lately?

The same party now plunders a poor nation's wealth to buy first class tickets for these boondoggles. The leader of the party, of course, watches all this, even as he points fingers and throws accusations at anyone else who dares criticise them.

No, the AAP's shenanigans are no longer funny. It is one of the saddest moments in Indian politics. For the dream has been shattered. The betrayal hurts. It is also uncomfortable to deal with, as it tells us that it wasn't just the fault of the Congress. Perhaps we as a nation are full of cheats, liars, thugs and plunderers. It's just a matter of getting the opportunity to do so.

When the AAP was on the streets, it hated conspicuous consumption and the waste of state resources. Once in power, it wants to travel first class and sample Bordeaux wines. This clearly shows that the idea of looting the nation never really troubled the AAP leaders. What bothered them was that they were not getting a chance to do so. Well, they have it now. Well done.

Already, several AAP ministers are tainted with charges ranging from faking degrees to corruption and rape. This abuse of office for personal luxury and gratification points clearly to the fact that the AAP has failed. In fact, it is likely to become, if not already, worse than the older political parties.

So what went wrong? Why did this Indian dream break? And what can we learn from it?

First, we created AAP when we were angry about the sheer magnitude of corruption in the political system. We somehow assumed that if there is a face we trust at the top, the party would cease to be corrupt. We were wrong. The lesson is this: to fix corruption, you need to make the government more accountable, not merely replace it or create new parties.

Second, the AAP's sheer desire to win cost them everything. In the last Delhi elections, they selected candidates based on just one factor—winnability. The biggest asset of the AAP, that they strove to represent the best in our society, was gone. In fact, good people were thrown out of the party. Looters, goons, rapists and frauds were invited in, as long as they could get some votes.

So the AAP won, but lost its ethical core—their values of integrity and honesty. And once the river is polluted, it is very hard to clean it again. Never compromise an organisation's core values, even if it means slower growth.

Finally, the lesson for us Indians is to not give up hope. Yes, AAP took us for a first-class ride. It is a bitter truth to face. It doesn't, however, mean that nothing can ever change in this country. We must move on and work to keep the government accountable, whichever party is in power.

For AAP, the only lesson is to acknowledge reality and fix itself. Calling Modi names isn't going to make things any better. Taking a hard look within might. Maybe they could do that on their first class flights, as they hover high above Delhi and sip some nice, Aam Aadmi vintage wine.

Uri Changed One Thing: India Is Never Going to Compare Itself with Pakistan

Using Pakistan to bolster its self-image cannot possibly do India any good

Imagine two kids in the same class of an elite school. Both kids come from poor backgrounds and are among the bottom rankers. Both fail often, but the first kid scores a few more marks than the second. The first kid feels good about this; at least he is doing better than the other one. The second kid hates himself, but lives for the occasional moment when he scores more than the first. They are both losers, but each is happy to compare himself with the other and feel better whenever possible.

However, things change over time. The first student's performance begins to improve. In time, he even reaches the top 10 in class. Meanwhile, the second student gets steadily worse in academics. He also joins a gang of bullies and starts taking drugs.

One day, a realisation dawns on the first student. He no longer wants to compare himself with this second student. The boy he revelled in beating once, now disgusts him. His only thought now is of emulating the class toppers.

In the analogy above, the first student is India and the second is Pakistan. Ever since Independence, we have loved to compare ourselves with Pakistan. It helped us cope with our Third-World status in the world. At least we were better than Pakistan. So, we took Pakistan seriously. Even though Pakistan was never able to build itself into a real country (it witnessed a military coup a decade into Independence, and then split into two pieces a decade after), *we* legitimised it. Pakistan was a failed state to begin with, but India needed it around because it reinforced her own political legitimacy. 'At least we are better off than Pakistan' is a rhetoric that worked for Indians for a very long time.

And then, something snapped. The Uri attack became the proverbial last straw, and India grew up overnight. We finally realised our self-worth. We understood that comparing ourselves to a student who comes last in class and is a certified bully is just not worth it.

India is today the fastest growing economy in the world. We have a functioning capital market, legal system, labour force, large consumer base and democracy. We would be stupid to not focus on what we have. Keeping the idea of Pakistan alive just to feel better about ourselves doesn't make sense anymore.

Pakistan was doomed from the start—a haphazard creation of a belligerent leader who preyed on the fears of the Muslim population. The British, reeling from the impact of the Second World War and in a hurry to leave, couldn't care less. Pakistan was created on the basis of a single emotion—fear of India's Hindus. It was essentially a giant refugee camp born out of irrational fear. Of course, such a setup was unlikely to create a strong country. It never did.

Also, since Pakistan was carved out in a hurry, they never had central structures and organised civil services like India's (such as the IAS or IPS) to help run the country. Adding to these misfortunes, its founder died within a year of its creation, leaving behind a leadership void and chaos. The army eventually took over, and things became worse. They have been, ever since.

Indians might say we never liked Pakistan. However, it was India that legitimised it the most, by inviting regime after regime for talks. This policy was only making things worse. It is still believed in some circles that India's Muslim vote bank does not want India to act tough against Pakistan. So Indian leaders wooed Pakistan, in a bid to woo the Muslim vote bank at home.

But it has all changed with the Uri attack; that was the tipping point. Indians—Hindus, Muslims and others—no longer feel sympathy for Pakistan. In fact, they feel disgust. Which country kills innocent people of other countries on a routine basis? Only Pakistan. No Indian today wants to be associated with it. And this is a major step in the growth of our national self-esteem. It is no longer defined in the context of Pakistan. That is setting our standards so low that it is almost an insult to ourselves.

India's lack of dependence on Pakistan to bolster its self-image hurts the latter most. For India is no longer interested in legitimising Pakistan. This will only speed up the disintegration of that country, barring an unlikely scenario where Pakistan's regime and its radical elements both turn over a new leaf. One feels bad for sane Pakistanis. In a land ruled by guns, they are powerless. Maybe the need of the hour there is the rise of a pro-India party. It may be against Pakistan's very DNA, but might be the only solution to its crisis.

However, the chances of Pakistan fixing itself are rather remote. And if it doesn't, the country could end up having to split again. It almost seems like that is Pakistan's karmic curse, for they caused a great nation to split once.

We, on the other hand, should congratulate ourselves as a nation. Not just for standing up to Pakistan or for the surgical strikes, but for finally growing up as a nation and realising our own value.

The Parable of PK: Having a Loud, Indecent Neighbour Calls for Out-of-the-box Solutions

India must look at fresh strategies to resolve the Kashmir dispute with Pakistan

Imagine you live in a colony of row houses. You have a big family with modest means. Somehow you make it work, taking everyone's needs and views into account. Your family's young generation is trying its best to come up in life, by working hard and staying optimistic despite adversities.

Imagine also that your immediate neighbour is PK. PK is poorer and less educated. PK doesn't run his house democratically, but rules with a stick. PK doesn't like to change.

PK watches you rise and sees that you have an even better future ahead of you. He notices that you now have a couple of cars in your garage. PK doesn't have any. Rather than emulate your progress, PK decides to do something else.

Regularly, he sneaks into your garage and deflates the tyres, smashes the glass or scratches the cars. PK does this at night, and then disappears. He then goes home, turns on his set-top box and watches TV, the only joy he has.

Since you are a respected, peace-loving member of the community, you try to deal with the situation in a decent manner. You request him not to do it. He doesn't listen. You invite him over for tea several times. He enjoys the tea, shakes hands, and continues his bad behaviour.

You go to his house with flowers to wish him on his birthday. He asks you in but damages your cars again the next day. You complain at the colony society meetings, where everyone advises you to remain calm and maintain peace. They give PK the same advice, but PK refuses to listen. He's even begun sending goons to scare you and your family.

Meanwhile, you are advised by self-styled 'experts' and 'secular pacifists' in your family to continue to talk to PK. Their solutions, if at all they offer them, range from evaluating the damage to the car and keeping the car covered to selling the car. If anyone else in the family proposes an out-of-the-box solution, the experts bash him.

The experts even say it is your fault. Why did you have to buy the car? Why did you make PK angry? Why didn't you send more flowers? Why don't you just give the car to him?

Meanwhile, PK continues his mischief. What are you to do?

In case you haven't guessed already, the above analogy refers to the Kashmir problem. You are India, PK is Pakistan, and the colony society is the UN. This conflict has been going on since Independence. Leader after leader, think-tank after think-tank, expert after expert, has failed to solve it. Meanwhile, the Kashmiri people continue to suffer; they live in danger and have no future to speak of.

The Indian Army has the tough job of keeping peace, sifting through the civilian population to apprehend militants. It gets a bad name every time it makes a mistake, and errors are inevitable with such an awful task. Our nation spend tens of thousands of crores every year just to keep Kashmir secure.

Hence, on Independence Day, you tried a different solution. You went and cut off the wires of the satellite dish of PK's set-top box. Every time he repaired it, you cut it off again. Frustrated, PK did not know what to do. After a while, you asked PK over for a chat. This time, he listened.

And this is what the PM did in his Independence Day speech. He expressed open support for the Balochistan movement. For our own sake, it is important for us Indians to understand the Baloch movement, understand why we are supporting it, and why we should back our government in doing so. This move will finally make our neighbour fall in line and listen to reason, accepting that one should not interfere in another country's internal strife, and that peace is what will finally lead to progress.

Balochistan is almost half the area of Pakistan, although, population-wise, it comprises less than 4 per cent of Pakistanis. Like Kashmiris—though the context and history are different—the Baloch people feel they were deprived of autonomy when the country was formed. They claim that Pakistan doesn't treat them fairly, that the army is oppressive, and that the Baloch deserve complete independence.

Make no mistake, the Baloch movement is violent and Pakistan identifies them as a terrorist group. However, one must also note that, in a country ruled with a gun, the opposition has to behave like a terrorist group too.

India must not fall into the trap of funding or backing violent attacks on innocent Pakistani civilians. Our Baloch support is strategic; it is a tactic aimed at getting Pakistan to stop interfering in Kashmir. If ending the oppression of the Baloch becomes a by-product of this strategy, it is even better.

India can help the Baloch give their cause global legitimacy, by extending political support and starting an anti-Pakistan PR campaign. Pakistan has a lot more to lose from Baloch independence than India would if it lost Kashmir (which India won't). If Balochistan splits away, Pakistan is literally cut in half and becomes much weaker.

If there is global consensus that (a) there is a humanitarian crisis in Balochistan and (b) Pakistan is a failed state that deserves to be split up to end global terrorism, nothing can stop the breakdown of Pakistan. Hence, it is in Pakistan's interest now to finally listen and cooperate in solving the Kashmir problem. We, on the other hand, must back the Baloch but we also need to be clear about the nature of the support we give them.

@chetan_bhagat

Chetan Bhagat Retweeted Imran Khan
Mr PM considering you wanted to be a beacon of peace, don't you think you needed to be more patient than attacking the moment things didn't go your way? Our people were killed, difficult to do a hugs session the day that happened isn't it? Don't give up if u r serious about peace

144 replies/ 439 retweets/ 2,198 likes

INDIANOMICS

Many felt having a stable government with a pro-business mindset in the centre would boost economic growth. However, this has not happened. The reasons behind this are analysed in 'Don't Let the 2014 Euphoria Turn into Despair'.

The government has made two moves that were much talked: the implementation of GST and demonetisation. 'Cracking the GST Puzzle' talks about why GST needs to be simplified in order to be successful. '28 Per Cent GST? At this Rate, India's Movie Biz Will Be a Flop Show' talks about how this tax has affected the film industry. But there is a reason why, despite criticism of these moves, Modi has so much support, and this is explained in 'The Three New I's of Indian Politics'.

'How to Tax with Love' and 'Suit-book Sarkar' talk about why it's important for the tax department not to treat taxpayers like criminals and why we need to stop seeing people who run businesses as criminals, and have a clear capitalistic policy.

Two government-run services are reviewed: public hospitals and Air India. In the light of the tragedy at Gorakhpur, 'The Government Is Bad At Running Hospitals, Let's Have Modicare' talks about how the Indian government can't handle complex services well and should relieve excess pressure on the public healthcare system and improve medical insurance coverage. Regarding Air India, 'Sell Air India for One Rupee' suggests we sell it, even if it's just for one rupee; in the long term, it will only save us a lot of money every year.

'It's Time to Analyse OROP with Our Heads, Not Our Hearts' talks about how we need to look at OROP with more clarity and see what we can do in the context of what is possible and affordable.

Lastly, the essay on Free Basics talks about how we should welcome it as a concept but also address the issues that it definitely has.

28 Per Cent GST? At this Rate, India's Movie Biz Will Be a Flop Show

Current GST rates have delivered a crushing blow to the Indian film industry

The Goods and Services Tax is finally here. It is a major reform that can streamline India's complicated indirect taxation system. Instead of multiple sales, service, entertainment, VAT, excise and octroi-like taxes, there will be one GST which would make accounting easier and remove taxes on taxes.

We also hope that the GST will reduce the impact of abrupt changes in industrial tax rates, which every budget so far has tinkered with. The expectation now is that, with a single GST, things will be more stable and, hence, more predictable.

Except, there is no one GST. It should perhaps be called GST5. For even in its introductory stage, the GST has five different rates: 0 per cent, 5 per cent, 12 per cent, 18 per cent and 28 per cent. Then there are the goods that fall outside the purview of these rates. And in a few cases, local bodies such as municipal corporations can impose their taxes on certain items too.

Hence, the GST5 is a halfway house to the final idea: to have, primarily, a single indirect tax rate for all goods and services in the country. Since that hasn't happened yet, various items have at present been placed in one of the five buckets.

The decision to do so is based on a mixture of common sense and the morality that we Indians love to bring to everything, including our tax rates. Hence, sinful items such as liquor and cigarettes are taxed higher. Fresh milk won't be taxed. However, UHT milk or milk sold in cartons will carry a tax of 5 per cent. Condensed milk will be taxed at 18 per cent.

The reasoning behind GST5 could be to ensure that the transition to a single GST rate is smooth and gradual. If one rate was decided on, it would lead to big changes in the prices of some items that were taxed at very different rates earlier. GST5 helps find rates that are close to those of the pre-GST era.

However, GST5 also poses problems. It leaves scope for a degree of arbitrariness in assigning rates to different items. And that creates scope for industry to lobby politicians to place their items in a lower tax bucket. It also makes certain industries uncompetitive. One such example is the film industry.

For some strange historical reason, watching movies in a theatre is seen as a luxury, a hedonistic pleasure that borders on sin. Little wonder, we have entertainment taxes as high as 100 per cent on movie ticket sales in some states.

These laws were made well before the era of television, let alone internet or digital entertainment. The current GST rate for cinema tickets is 28 per cent, on par with gambling. Moreover, local bodies can further tax cinemas, increasing the burden on ticket buyers. Meanwhile, your set-top box subscription will be taxed at 18 per cent. So for some bizarre reason, the government wants to charge you more if you watch a movie in a theatre than on your TV at home. And, of course, many who watch pirated content pay absolutely nothing.

In this scenario, the film industry is the one that's getting penalised above all. There are no logical reasons for this, only flimsy ones such as: (a) these filmi types are so rich anyway (not true: wages across the industry are meagre, barring a few powerful people); (b) films make so much money, look at *Baahubali* (not true: only 10 per cent of the films released in India are hits); and (c) why should we care about such an unnecessary industry anyway (we should, because it has a huge impact on our economy and around the world).

Due to such unreasonable biases, we have hit the industry with a tax rate that will render it uncompetitive. For every ticket sold, a high GST would be deducted. And nearly half of what remains will go to the theatre owner. After that, there will be a distributor margin of 10–20 per cent. Whatever is left (say, 25–30 per cent) will go to the makers of the film. TV and subscribed digital content have neither such high taxes nor so many middlemen. Also, compared to TV, piracy is more common in films.

In other words, this current structure can only mean one thing—the eventual decline of India's film industry, whether in terms of overall profitability, volume of output, or revenues.

As content becomes more easily available on your phone or TV, the incentive to go to the theatre to watch movies will no doubt be drastically reduced. And even if people do go, most of what they pay will be eaten up by taxes and middlemen.

This doesn't leave filmmakers with much business. Sure, there will be the occasional superstar movie that does wonders at the box office. But exceptions do not make an industry. A healthy, regular output does. The film industry drives our country's economy in a big way. When people come to theatres, they step out of their homes and do more retail shopping. Films also drive our music industry. Finally, they represent a key part of Brand India to the world.

Overall, the bigger issue is to move GST5 to GST1. We need one reasonable GST rate that covers every good and service in the country. Until that happens, the government would do well to move the film industry to a lower tax bucket, so that it remains competitive and continues to entertain us for years to come.

Post this article, the tax rate for movie tickets above ₹100 was brought down to 18 per cent.

Don't Let the 2014 Euphoria Turn into Despair

While cleaning up India's economy, the government would do well to opt for smooth transitions rather than strict penalties

GDP growth data is like a grade in the government's report card, at least in intellectual circles. This grade is for a core subject: the economy. The Narendra Modi government is being subjected to a particularly harsh assessment on this test. After all, many saw this government as a compromise on secularism, the price we needed to pay for strong economic growth.

'Yes, the BJP has a communal ring to it, but who cares, if they can make India rich,' was how many non-traditional BJP voters justified their votes for Modi in May 2014. These voters led the BJP to a big victory, and we got a stable, right-wing government. Many thought the Indian economy would now fly. People expected the fiery Gujarati entrepreneurial spirit to reach the PMO, a departure from the slow, soft-spoken, academic style of Manmohan Singh. The 'nayi bahu' excitement around Modi was unprecedented. And as anyone who has gone through the 'my nayi bahu is the best' phase will attest, when you expect so much, some disappointment is bound to follow.

Yashwant Sinha's 2017 open letter on the economy had relatively few defenders outside the BJP. Objectively speaking, it was low on data. It was also somewhat alarmist, predicting an extremely unlikely 'crash landing'. However, it did make the point that this turbo-powered government may have underperformed in a core area— the economy.

There is no denying that India's GDP growth continues to slow down. Given our low base, we should have been close to a 10 per cent annual growth rate by now. So why are we at 5.7 per cent (or 3.7 per cent, according to some)? This hasn't hurt the BJP politically yet, given that the masses don't track GDP like the experts. However, once there's a media perception that this government cannot deliver growth (and hence jobs), the message will trickle down. This would destroy the roaring tiger image of the Modi government and advance the (embarrassing) possibility that the Manmohan Singh government, for all its policy paralysis, could deliver better on growth. That's bound to hurt the BJP's chances in 2019.

Little wonder then that the government went into defensive mode, calling out naysayers and pessimists. Naturally, it is concerned about the self-fulfilling nature of economic pessimism. If everyone believes times are bad, tightens their purse strings and reduces spending, then the economy does indeed suffer. Euphoria 2014 becomes Doubts 2017 which, in the worst-case scenario, turns into Despair 2018, and so on.

How did this happen? Is it due to specific measures like note-bandi and GST? Or is it something about the government's attitude that is hurting the economy, these measures being just a manifestation? Chances are that it is the latter.

When Modi came to power, entrepreneurs across the country believed in him. His energy, zeal, hard work and belief in India continue to be inspiring in some ways. However, the BJP government seems to have become obsessed with one thing—black money.

In our country, a lot of black money holders have done business for decades in a culture of tax evasion. These people, a few hundred thousands of them, control our economy, creating millions of legitimate jobs and adding billions to the GDP. What do we do in this situation? Suffocate them, and the jobs they create, to death? Or do we live with both the good and the bad they represent, and softly move them towards a cleaner system? Should we teach them a lesson for being bad, and risk businesses shrinking and jobs disappearing? Or should we come up with easier ways to make the transition so that ways of doing business in our country get cleaned up over time?

There are no easy answers. However, GDP data indicates that this government may have been a bit too strict. Today, the entrepreneur fears the taxman. Nobody wants to take big risks to grow in this atmosphere of fear, despite assurances from the tax department that they will refrain from unnecessary harassment. There are so many new rules that, if someone wants to make a businessman's life difficult in this country, they can. And if the entrepreneur goes into consolidation mode, we will have an economic slowdown for sure.

The government also seems to have fallen behind on the concept of 'change management'. When you are making life difficult for people, you have to give them incentives to accept the discomfort. If the GST switchover was going to be cumbersome, the least the government could do was to reduce rates drastically in the 'change management' phase. Instead, for many products and services, rates were higher than before.

Noble intentions to clean India up are not enough to ensure that people cooperate through the change. Every transition, even if it's for the greater good, has to be managed well. The government needs entrepreneurs if it wants the economy to grow in double digits. Teaching them a lesson may be justified but, sadly, it will hamper growth. Taxes should be kept low, as getting through the transition smoothly is more important than penalising defaulters. Instead of playing the strict teacher trying to get the homework done, the government would do better to slowly turn them into motivated students who want to do their own homework.

@chetan_bhagat

Hate Modi or BJP. You have the right to. But think twice before painting Congress in pure gold. Don't forget massive scams in their time, where spectrum, coal and even games weren't spared.Citizens have to make a choice during elections, but then must keep all parties accountable

1,936 replies/ 5,854 retweets/ 16,735 likes

@chetan_bhagat

Petrol Diesel prices too high. Said it before saying it now. Taxation on fuel needs to be revisited. People are suffering. Inflation will rise. Why not just simply bring it under GST?

440 replies/ 843 retweets/ 5,170 likes

Cracking the GST Puzzle

It's a modern reform implemented with an archaic sarkari attitude, so here are five ways to set it right

Confession: My brain is fried right now. Reason: I have spent the last several hours trying to figure out the Indian government's GST return filing processes. I am still somewhat confused. This, when I have a business degree, worked at an investment bank for a decade, and analysed hundreds of annual reports for companies.

Ask any tax expert in the country and they would agree. The GST puzzle is so complex that it feels like a cruel and nerdy prank played by taxmen on India's entrepreneurs. It would be funny, if it wasn't real and didn't threaten millions of businesses and jobs across the nation.

The technically complex design of the GST returns process assumes that every businessman in the country is an experienced Munimji and entrepreneurs have nothing better to do (such as running their businesses) than fill out multiple puzzle-like GST forms every month. So while an American business may be figuring out how to make app-based sales or invest in new technologies, the poor Indian business is busy scrambling to figure out and meet three (yes, three!) monthly deadlines for GST returns.

It is a classic case of tax nerds imposing their jargon on helpless users. The tax department continues to say they want to be more taxpayer-friendly, but they have always lacked customer focus—evident in their process design which assumes that users have advanced taxation expertise. Small wonder, then, that GST is fast becoming unpopular.

This is unfortunate because this tax reform actually has the power to change India. For a few silly reasons stemming from sarkari attitude issues, the entire GST programme risks failure. The only silver lining is the fact that the GST council continues to meet and revise its processes. This at least shows a willingness to take feedback. If that is indeed the case, here are some practical suggestions to save GST's reputation and India's economy.

One, GST rates are too many. The more rates there are, the more complex the forms and processes get, and the more discretion the authorities get to tinker around. This is the complete antithesis of what GST set out to do. There needs to be only one GST rate, and an exempt list. If you are itching for more rates, just have two. No more.

Two, the GST rates are too high. There are too many items in the 28 per cent category, and even 18 per cent is too much. Right now, input cost GST reductions are not being passed to consumers, and probably won't be for a few years to come. Hence, GST rates need to be reduced considerably for the medium term. The government must note that, for many who pay income tax, GST comes out of post-tax income. To gouge people is to upset people. The ideal GST for the moment would be 10 per cent flat for almost all goods, with a higher rate of 15 per cent for some items, if absolutely necessary.

Three, the 'pleasure equals more taxes' attitude has to go. To tax air-conditioned venues or readymade garments more as they are luxuries is archaic, obsolete and fake-socialist. After all, people should be free to spend their post-tax income however they want. Should I sweat to deserve a lower GST? Really?

Four, GST returns are too complex. The government has an ambitious plan of tracking every invoice for every transaction for every business in the country, and matching the GST collected and paid on these every month. While this may be a dream for the tax department, it makes life super-complicated for entrepreneurs, many of whom have never done this their entire lives.

A simpler method is to go by aggregate cash outflows and inflows of GST, and arrive at a net number on a quarterly basis (unless a business specifically wants monthly refunds). In other words, a businessman says: I paid this amount in GST, and I collected this amount; hence the net amount due to/from the government is this much. That's it.

Right now you have three returns a month, every month, with multiple complicated entries that have to be matched with every buyer and seller you did business with. Google the GST F5 form for Singapore, a simple quarterly online form with just fourteen boxes to fill. It can be that simple. (Oh, and Singapore's GST is 7 per cent flat. Just saying.)

Finally, just do not hold on to Indian attitudes from the 1960s, which would have us believe that (a) profits

are terrible; (b) all businesses are run by crooks who
have to be caught red-handed; (c) running businesses is
no work, so people can sit around and file returns all
day; and (d) tax guys must behave like colonial lagaan
collectors, hunting down businessmen who are no better
than uncouth thieves.

There is no reason to disdain or damage Indian
businesses. India's private sector is our lifeblood. Without
them, many Indian households would not be able to run.
Take your taxes by all means, but in reasonable amounts
and in a simple manner. Don't suffocate Indian enterprise.

The GST reforms, when fully in place, can truly make
India a more competitive player in the business world.
Right now, however, it's a modern reform mixed with
old-fashioned attitudes, and the latter risk damaging
GST's reputation. Hope the authorities address this
problem, so that they can truly celebrate and raise a
toast to GST's success one day (but don't forget to pay
GST on the toast!).

The Government Is Bad at Running Hospitals, Let's Have Modicare Instead

Relieving excess pressure on the public healthcare system and improving medical insurance coverage could avert tragedies like Gorakhpur in the future

In one of the most tragic and macabre incidents in recent times, seventy children died in BRD Medical College Hospital in Gorakhpur in a span of two days. The supplier allegedly stopped supplies of liquid oxygen to the hospital, citing multiple unpaid bills. Many theories were floated to explain this mishap. Blame was ascribed to the government, the hospital authorities, and the supplier. Some even said this wasn't about the oxygen shortage at all. Essentially, everyone involved found someone to blame.

The children, however, are dead. Their families will have to live with this irreparable loss and immeasurable sorrow all their lives. What makes things worse is the knowledge that this was avoidable. This happened because of one reason—utter mismanagement, the hallmark of a range of government-run services in India. Those who remember the pre-cell phone era will recall the harrowing experience of trying to obtain a landline connection. Government-run hotels and airlines are usually of far poorer quality than their private counterparts.

In short, when it comes to the Indian government, one thing is clear: it just can't handle complex services well. When the operations require constant interaction with multiple customers, quick decision-making and certain standards of quality control, the government's performance is simply terrible.

Of course, mismanagement at MTNL means you have to wait endlessly for a phone, and at Air India, it would mean your flight gets delayed. But when things are bungled up in a government hospital, you could die—even en masse, as in this case.

The purpose of this article is not government-bashing; there's more than enough of that going around. It is to make the government understand and accept its limitations—the fact that it just can't do complex services. The reason is simple. Most government staff adopt a 'cover-their-backside' approach to work. For government employees, there is no incentive for initiative, creativity or improving status quo. In fact, when new ideas go wrong, they suffer for it. Hence, the typical babu's approach is this: do nothing new. Repeat, until retired.

This is why nobody at BRD Medical College Hospital in Gorakhpur acted on something as basic as oxygen. Ideally, the oxygen supplier should be on autopay. The hospital should also have an oxygen inventory system. Drops in oxygen stores should trigger a fresh order, with automatic payments. Every government hospital should have a line of credit for pre-approved emergency items.

These are fairly obvious, implementable remedies for the existing state of affairs. However, who will do this?

Nobody suggesting such measures would get a raise, a promotion or any other form of recognition for doing so. However, if for some reason there are hiccups, the individual will be blamed and punished (with a bad transfer, perhaps, or a delayed promotion) by the system. Hence, do nothing.

A better solution is to change this management style across government entities. Our government officials need to be empowered or incentivised to improve things.

The government must also take note of its limitations. While it doesn't do complex services well, it does run fairly decent financial institutions. For instance, LIC is one of India's top insurers. Money is a simpler product to handle than, say, liquid oxygen and life-saving medicines because routine systems suffice to keep things going. The government could harness it strengths in this area to improve healthcare by taking on a more active role in India's medical insurance scene, for instance, and be less involved in running hospitals.

Do note that some of India's best doctors are in government hospitals. Talent does get attracted to government jobs and often stays on. However, it is the running of the hospitals—cleanliness, supplies, logistics and payments—where the government falters. Get out of that slump. Insure more people. Give them good coverage plans. Hold on to those good doctors. And let more private players run the hospitals.

Some government initiatives like the Rural Health Insurance Scheme have been modestly successful, but they have not transformed the medical sector. The insurance coverage offered by such schemes is paltry. A new comprehensive medical insurance scheme (and it doesn't have to be free) that offers Indians good coverage across the private as well as public health network may work better than the present system where the government runs thousands of large hospitals. If there can be Obamacare, why not Modicare?

One really needs to relieve the excess pressure on the public health system. Speaking of tragedies like Gorakhpur, while some fault lies with poor management, a lot is owing to overstretched healthcare facilities. Whether in terms of better insurance schemes or new hospitals, we do need to spend more on healthcare (a sizeable percentage of the GDP).

Nothing can lessen the pain of the people who lost their kids. What we can hope for is that lessons are learnt from this horrible incident and our healthcare system is reformed, so that Gorakhpur never, ever happens again.

Sell Air India for One Rupee: Right Now, It's a Giant Black Hole Relentlessly Sucking in Taxpayer Money

Air India will never make enough money to pay off its debts; it's high time the government sold it to the highest private bidder

In 2017, the Cabinet gave in-principle approval to sell Air India. It is an oft-repeated idea, but this time the resolve seems to be stronger. The government will really be doing our country a huge favour if it gets rid of this company which is a giant black hole that relentlessly sucks in taxpayer money.

As an ex-distressed banker, I can say this: some companies can be rescued from the hole they have dug themselves in. Others have dug it so deep, they can never, ever get out. Air India is in the latter category. There is no point saying, 'But last time I flew, the service was good.' It's irrelevant. The hard truth is this: the company is a dud. Sorry.

Here's the math, in the form of an example. Imagine your neighbour has a drinking problem because of which he racks up loans of over ₹5 crore. But instead of earning money and paying his debts, he continues to borrow even more and spends another ₹70 lakhs a year on his addiction. Over the decades, you have rescued him several times. However, he refuses to change. Now the loans are simply too big. Even if he tries his best, he can't make more than a couple of lakhs a year. Hence, he can never repay his debts.

To understand Air India, multiply the numbers in the example above by 10,000. It has over ₹50,000 crore of debt and is cash flow negative, reportedly by over ₹7,000 crore a year. The numbers could be worse, as the company hasn't released recent data, not to mention the fact that the CAG has raised issues about the existing data.

Even in the best of scenarios, Air India won't earn enough to repay its debt. So no new buyer can purchase it as-is, with its mountain of debt. There is simply no scope to repay it. Financially speaking, right now, Air India is the worst corporate in the country.

There's no point in casting blame. When sins have accumulated over decades, no one person or set of persons is to blame. One does feel bad for the 20,000 plus employees, though, who may even be working hard at running the company from day to day.

But the black hole is going to remain just that, and the taxpayer is paying for it. Air India's annual cash flow loss is equal to what Vijay Mallya's Kingfisher Airlines owes the banks. Air India costs us one Mallya a year, money that can be used to build hundreds of hospitals and schools.

Among the many lame arguments against selling Air India is the one that reminds us that it is the flag carrier. Well, many countries no longer have flag carriers (including America). In other cases, they don't cost their governments so much. Flag carrier pride in a passenger airline is stupid. Air India is not the Indian Air Force.

Air India's role in rescue efforts is also tom-tommed by these naysayers. Well, it beats all logic to keep such an expensive operation on standby for occasional rescues. It is a better idea for the Centre to give money to private airlines in such emergencies. Do we really think that in the event of a rare, genuine calamity, if the government wants to pay to hire a plane for rescue operations, IndiGo and SpiceJet are going to refuse? And isn't this far more efficient than burning ₹7,000 crore a year?

These two noble arguments hide the real reason we're keeping Air India alive. It is the netas' and babus' club in the sky. Politicians and bureaucrats, along with their families, friends and neighbours, abuse Air India to get free upgrades and slavish service from the staff. Taking Air India off the government's hands will end these VVIP joys.

Even if we want to pamper netas and babus, there are cheaper ways. Paying them money to fly business or even first class in private airlines will be less expensive than keeping the Air India monster alive. The government can buy upgrade vouchers for its senior functionaries.

So how does one sell Air India? Its assets, office infrastructure, running operations and landing rights have some value, though well below its debt. The government should give it to the highest bidder among various private players. Of course, the bid is unlikely to pay off the entire debt, so the winning bidder will probably be someone who wants the least discount on the loan.

Employees may be retained or retrenched; that is up to the buyer to decide. But a decent retrenchment package (say, three years' salary) for the entire staff would cost around ₹9,000 crore (given a salary bill of ₹3,000 crore a year). The new buyers will take that into account in their bid.

Even in an ideal scenario, the government will have to give a discount on the loan. It may even have to give the company to the new buyer for one rupee. The sale will not make the government any money. But it will get rid of a part of the loan and the whole cash-burning enterprise. To that extent, this exercise would be not so much a sale of Air India as good riddance. This is something we need to understand going into the transaction, so we don't have unrealistic expectations from it.

Beware opposing voices that will complain about the sale, 'We sold Air India for nothing.' Tell them: we didn't sell it, we got rid of it, and that will save us a lot of money every year.

Let's all keep up the pressure to ensure that the Modi government sells Air India. We will be doing the country's finances a big favour.

@chetan_bhagat

Am all for fiscal prudence but to overtax fuel and then spend thousands of crores paying for Air India's losses and funding bank NPAs also doesn't seem to be the best way to do things.

94 replies/ 190 retweets/ 1,028 likes

@chetan_bhagat

A bit surprised that skill based certificate programs offered by educational institutions are subject to 18% GST. Most countries don't have it. Govt should consider making education GST free.

249 replies/ 1,060 retweets/ 4,716 likes

How to Tax with Love

These are ten ways the income tax department can reform itself to get taxpayer buy-in

Startling income tax data was in the news in 2016: only 1.2 crore Indians (one per cent of the population) pay income taxes. Checks with the tax department revealed that the data was somewhat unrepresentative, as it only considered taxes on salaries. The number of individuals paying taxes is close to five crores or 4 per cent of the population.

At the same time, the tax department did confirm that the number of individuals claiming to have an annual income greater than ₹50 lakh is only 150,000, in a country of 120 crore people. Note that modest two-bedroom apartments in Mumbai suburbs alone cost ₹3 crore. One wonders who is buying them, isn't it?

Hence, the tax department's assertion that there is a significant amount of tax evasion in the country may not be incorrect. And the so-called hostility with which our tax officials approach taxpayers is somewhat justified. They could argue that they would not have to be so rough if people only behaved.

At the same time, there are constant reports of genuine taxpayers claiming harassment and persecution by tax officials. The tax department, many income earners say, starts with the assumption that the taxpayer is in the wrong, deliberately complicates rules, and comes after you only because you decided to pay your taxes (while ignoring or remaining blissfully unaware of the real tax evaders).

As the Indian economy gets bigger, invites more foreign investment, and tries to expand its tax base, some things need to change about the way the tax department does its job. It is one of the few government departments that is in constant touch with citizens. If it continues to operate in an archaic and hostile manner, the benefits of policy reforms will never accrue to the economy. Here are ten concrete, doable ways the income tax department can tax, but with love.

First, treat the taxpayer as a customer. The current tax department mentality is to act like the police and approach the taxpayer as a criminal, guilty unless proven otherwise. It is tough for people to part with their money. The last thing you should do while taking it from them is to be ungracious about it. Without the taxpayer, the government can't function. Seeing the taxpayer as a customer means taking constant feedback, having service benchmarks (turnaround times, for example), and not presuming guilt.

Second, simplify forms. The government has tried but sadly failed to do this. The Indian tax department should download some forms from the Hong Kong or Singapore tax department websites. These are some of the simplest and most effective tax forms in the world. Please emulate them.

Third, design a good, robust and modern website. India is the land of IT companies. Hire a good company to revamp your customer interface. Again, if you see the taxpayer as a customer, you will approach the website differently. The layout, the downloads, and the language used, should all change. Yes, get an app too.

Fourth, good quality paper. Current tax department communication seems stuck in the 1980s, with cheap super-thin sheets and envelopes, and poor-quality black and white printing. Come on. We are one of the world's top economies.

Fifth, simpler nomenclature. Terms like ITR4 and 26AS intimidate people. Sit down one day, and rename and reorganise all the forms that have been amended and cluttered with complex nomenclature over the years. It's scary enough to pay taxes. Don't make it scarier.

Sixth, say thanks and mean it. People who pay taxes are nation-builders. Seeing all rich people as thieves is a throwback to the evil-landlord-and-poor-peasant movies of the 1970s. You don't only become rich by stealing from the poor. You could also generate wealth from creativity, innovation, hard work and enterprise. How can you punish people for that? The top 10 per cent of the country's taxpayers should actually get a nice letter and memento (not cheap quality, please!) from the IT department.

Seventh, don't send scary letters. Yes, the department officials are under pressure to increase revenue. However, you cannot scare taxpayers. For instance, the kind of letters that say, 'We believe that, the way things are going, you should make 20 per cent more money this year, so we hope you will (and you'd better) pay that much more tax.' Really? Do we need to be so intimidating?

Eighth, set up tax guidance centres. People should have a place to go to figure out how to do their taxes, where they don't need to hire a private advisor. Organise taxpayer training at enquiry and guidance centres that run well. Again, make sure they're nice. They should not be like sarkari torture chambers with endless waits and creaky fans. This is the last government department that can claim it doesn't have money.

Ninth, share macro data. Without revealing individual details, macro data should be shared with the public to enable us to understand how tax collections are going.

Tenth, tell taxpayers how their money is being used. Of course, funds are amalgamated at the top. However, it would be nice to hear that the tax I paid last year helped make this road.

As Veda Vyasa said in the Mahabharata, a king should collect taxes like a bee collects nectar from flowers—painlessly. It is about time we behaved like a modern, world-class economy when it comes to tax collection and learned to tax with love.

'Suit-boot Sarkar' Doesn't Want the Rest Suited and Booted

The country needs a shift from pseudo-socialism to a healthy capitalism in its government policies

So, it is official. We are a socialist country. When the so-called right-wing and pro-business party delivers a populist budget, with an eye on the fattest vote banks (the rural poor and the farmers this time), you know India is a long way from being a capitalist nation.

Many experts have analysed the 2016 budget. The positives, most agree, are a certain restraint in keeping fiscal spending in check, and a push to rural infrastructure. The glaring negative is the lack of big ideas which could truly transform our economy, spur new investment, and create jobs.

The government seems to have forgotten its poll promises, particularly to the educated youth of this country. The middle class—the hardworking, tax-paying millions (who ironically supported the BJP in the last election)—were gouged further. It must have been a rude shock to learn that their pension savings would be hit with another tax, not to mention a few more surcharges and cesses, scraping out their already-lighter wallets. In other words, this was not a BJP budget. It was a UPA cut-and-paste budget. Worse, it was one of the lacklustre UPA budgets. If the BJP had been in Opposition, they would have criticised this budget. They would have called it dull, boring, populist, anti-business and anti-middle class.

Well, such is political life. You promise voters something before the election and they vote for you. Then you don't need them anymore, and you ignore them. This is what the Congress did. This is what the BJP is doing. It is just sad that the BJP didn't even spare two of its most loyal supporters in the 2014 polls—India Inc and the youth.

Why did the BJP do this? It lost a few state elections. So it sat down and did the math. Farmers and poor people are greater in number. So let's target them this time, it decided. Let's create a poor vs rich and poor vs middle class divide. In other words, let's not talk about a good Indian budget, which is good for all, rich and poor. No, we must always milk the poor vs rich narrative, and then skin the middle class and the rich some more.

Sounds familiar? Well, the Congress has done it quite successfully in the past. Had it not been for the monumental scams, this narrative might even have kept them in power. AAP is trying to do it, and is quite good at it as well. Now the BJP is trying to do it too, and letting down the country's youth and the business community quite shamefully in the process.

The party's over: India's youth will need millions of new jobs in coming years. Where will they come from?

For business is still hard to do in India. For example, try to open a small café in Mumbai. You may be passionate about serving good food, but unless you're passionate about hustling the BMC and half-a-dozen other government entities for permissions, you had better give up. Even if you do open that café, your middle-class customers will be taxed on the bill amount, which they pay from their already-taxed income. Thus, they will think ten times about eating out, especially since their car runs on petrol that is taxed at over 100 per cent, despite oil prices being at historic lows.

The politician will say, but why should I care for these café owners and middle-class diners when I have millions of poor people to think about? Well, when you make business hard and dining out unaffordable with your taxes, there will be no café. When there is no café, there are no jobs at the café. When there are no jobs at the cafe, many of those poor people stay jobless. Thus, overtaxing business and middle-class consumption actually harms the poor. It, in fact, keeps them poor.

What we call pro-poor in India is usually pro-poverty. Capitalism works on the premise of incentivising private individuals to make money, and thus increases consumption as well as jobs. However, no political party in India believes in this, for socialism is a much easier sell. Even for a right-wing party like the BJP. They don't want to be tagged as a suit-boot ki sarkar. So they have joined the rest in making policies that ensure India never gets suited or booted.

A rags-to-riches Indian billionaire once told me, 'In India, we are now habituated to being poor.' Maybe he was right. Poverty can be addictive.

As for the youth of this country, the ones who still have dreams and want India to give them the opportunities to fulfil them ... sorry, we are not ready yet. There's still too many of us who believe in poverty and socialism. No neta will go against that tide, no matter what they say in their poll speeches.

So, if you really want change, don't just back a political leader or party. Spread the message of good and fair capitalism in this country. Until enough people are convinced that this is the way to go, no politician will ever do anything about it. In the meantime, try to get a job. There aren't going to be many of them going around in the next few years. And whether the BJP will have a job in 2019 or not, well, that's another discussion, isn't it?

@chetan_bhagat

Chetan Bhagat Retweeted Elon Musk
The govt should note that the world's biggest CEOs of
the most innovative companies want to be in India but
find the regulations too hard. They bring with them
investments and jobs. Regulations must not be a hurdle
to that.

97 replies/ 517 retweets/ 1,976 likes

Free Basics May Not Be Totally on the Mark, But Don't Trash It

Initiatives to open the internet up to more people
around the world must be encouraged
while addressing legit concerns about
free and full access

Before I begin, let me confess that I am a bit of a Mark Zuckerberg fan. Who wouldn't be? Harvard dropout creates internet startup, and turns it into one of the most valuable companies in the world. Facebook has a billion-and-a-half-plus active subscribers. People are addicted to FB, where they can spend hours every day tracking their friends' lives. Mark changed the world in the coolest way imaginable. He never forced anyone. Yet, he attracted everyone to his creation. Soon, he became a billionaire. Then, he did something even cooler. He pledged 99 per cent of his $45 billion fortune to charity. It's a staggering amount (around ₹300,000 crore) to give away. All this, and Mark is only thirty-four. I think, for all practical purposes, he is the coolest person alive.

Why is this important? It is because Mark is backing an initiative called Free Basics (earlier known as internet. org) which will supposedly help connect more people in the world to the net. Free Basics involves collaborating with existing telecom companies in developing countries where internet penetration is still low. Telecom companies already connect people in these countries with voice services on the phone. Many such people cannot afford data services, so they are cut off from the world of the internet. A quick way to connect them is to offer them free internet, customised to a few chosen sites which will be designed for lower bandwidths. The telecom companies and site owners will work out between them how the subsidy is absorbed.

So far so good. Who can argue with poor people being given free internet access? Even if it's slower, it's better than nothing, right? Even if Free Basics only allows you to visit a few sites, isn't it better than not having access to any sites? But this is where it gets tricky. This limited range of sites is at the core of the opposition to Free Basics. Which are those sites (FB is the main one, of course)? Who will be the gatekeeper that selects those sites (FB seems to be the one)? If only a few sites are allowed, won't owners of excluded sites suffer as they would then have a smaller user base? Won't the new netizens be denied competitive choices—online retail options and media content, for instance?

These are real issues. Thankfully, the internet has not been regulated so far in terms of which site will be allowed which customers. Imagine Google being asked by regulators to pay up for every net user they reach in India. Just like spectrum, what if internet user access begins to get sold? It is possible. But it will kill the internet as we know it. Right now, any small startup can hope to create a killer website and reach the entire world (Facebook did exactly that).

If governments or corporations regulate user access, only the big players can dominate the internet. They already do, but this domination isn't imposed or coercive. You choose Facebook, and that's what makes it cool. The Free Basics initiative, though cool in its intentions to connect the world, lacks coolness when it restricts the sites available to users. It also sets a dangerous precedent, for soon it will be okay to make only a certain part of the internet available to a certain set of users (based on pricing, the location of your country, and so on).

Free Basics proponents counter these charges with: how does limited access matter when we are providing internet access for free? Those who want the whole range of sites (essentially, access to the entire internet) can always take a paid plan. Besides, exposure to a few sites will only whet the user's appetite for more internet, and they are likely to buy a data plan sooner rather than later. Also, in a free market, if Facebook or any other company tries a monopolistic stunt, it will be exposed. These are valid arguments too.

Overall, Free Basics has issues. However, to throw the idea away altogether doesn't seem to make sense either. A lack of understanding of this complex project has led to Free Basics opponents painting Mark as a control freak and Facebook as the evil MNC empire. Its PR blitz (somewhat over the top, with expensive ads featuring poor farmers) alone has created detractors.

'Such expensive ads show there must be an ulterior motive' is not really a logical statement, however. There are win-win situations too, in life, and one can probably trust Mark more than many other businessmen out there.

We should welcome Free Basics as a concept, but we need to bring out the concerns as well. Given the huge social welfare implications of this project along with the business opportunity it presents, a great solution can and must be hammered out. Facebook should feel secure about opening up the internet because there is little doubt that, even with universal access, people will spend most of their time on FB. We netizens, on the other hand, need to accept that if Facebook is leading the initiative, they deserve to get some reasonable benefits out of it.

Our government is certainly not able to provide internet services on the scale envisioned by such projects. Involving the private sector is thus necessary and inevitable in our country. From public transport apps to free internet providers, such initiatives should be welcomed, not painted as villains. We must also, however, iron out any legitimate concerns that may be raised about them. Free Basics is welcome, Mark, but only with a bit of free, basic common sense.

It's Time to Analyse OROP with Our Heads, Not Our Hearts

The 'one rank, one pension' scheme for our defence forces needs to be objectively debated in the public domain

Few government professions in India enjoy as much public goodwill as our defence forces. Mention the Indian Army (for the purpose of this article, army includes all forces—air force and navy as well) and our chests swell with pride. The army is an apolitical body that works well and quietly, and does a great job protecting our borders from some of our not-so-friendly neighbours. Even in times of domestic trouble, such as riots or floods, the army is called in and things begin to get better.

In combat, or during encounters with terrorists, our soldiers often lay down their lives or suffer grievous injuries in the line of duty. With all this selfless sacrifice, it is not difficult to see why the army enjoys so much support from our civilian population. Our popular culture, especially films and songs, mostly shows the army in a positive light (unlike the police and politicians). Media coverage, too, focusses on their sacrifice and hard work.

While this positive image is great, it can cloud an objective analysis of how we manage our defence resources in certain situations. One such issue is the OROP scheme. While OROP means 'one rank, one pension', it is a bit of a misnomer. It actually refers to one rank, the latest, and the highest pension for that rank, irrespective of when you retired. Army veterans essentially want an upward pension revision system for all veterans in the country or their surviving spouses, estimated to be around 3.2 million in number today.

There are several reasons why their demand is justified. Pension discrepancy between an officer who retired in 1990 and an equal-ranked officer who retired in 2015 can be dramatic. A certain consistency is required, especially since the army intrinsically believes in the concept of rank, and allows its officers to retain their ranks even after retirement. Many political parties had also promised OROP in their election manifestos, so the government had to deliver at some point. Popular and social media largely sided with the veterans, with arguments ranging from 'they guard our borders so we should give them what they want' to 'how can we disrespect our soldiers'.

Somewhere in all this, things became too simplistic. The army was good and the veterans were always right. The political class and the government were stingy, greedy and insensitive. After all, those who protect our borders must be treated well. OROP was seen as a way to ensure that our soldiers are justly rewarded for their services. Hence, you better give OROP, and now!

People who recommended an objective analysis had to scurry and hide in a corner. For nobody would hear a word against OROP, and with the veterans protesting in the nation's capital, even the government was pushed to a corner. OROP was announced. The government estimated a liability of around ₹12,000 crore per year from its implementation. However, the veterans are still not happy, as they feel many of their demands are not met by the present scheme.

What should we do? Should we maintain the 'Army Good, Politician Bad' argument? Should we still say 'give them whatever they want because they guard our borders' (by the way, paramilitary forces like the BSF are not eligible for OROP)? Or should we at least look into the various aspects of OROP and, dare we say, its pros and cons?

We should. For, in a country of limited resources like India, an expense as big as OROP must be examined carefully and kept within limits. At present, our defence budget is ₹250,000 crore. In addition, we pay defence pensions amounting to ₹60,000 crore per year. OROP will add another ₹12,000 crore to this expenditure annually. Note that these pensions are, by definition, for services already rendered. Nothing is obtained in return for this outlay.

While we all agree we should treat our army personnel well, what's the best course of action in this situation? To pay the veterans more, or to pay new hires in the army more? To increase the salaries of the officers, or those of the jawans? To invest in recruiting better talent, or in creating more jobs? Should money be spent on pensions, or more hospitals for veterans? Should war-affected veteran families be paid different pensions from those who retired safe and sound? As a solution to increased pension expense, can veterans be re-hired in certain jobs that are useful to the economy? Also, if we have OROP for the army, why not for our paramilitary forces and police? Can we afford to pay them all?

All these issues make OROP more complex than it seems, and it is high time we had a sane, objective debate about it, rather than an emotional, army-is-amazing-so-just-give-it-everything one. Forget OROP, many sectors don't even have pensions. Sure, a certain form of rank and pay equalisation needs to happen so that things don't fall too far apart. However, it has to be done in the context of what is possible and affordable, and after analysing what alternative welfare those funds can actually provide as well as the precedent it will set for similar schemes. Only then will we reach a sensible conclusion on OROP. We love our army with all our hearts, but it's time we thought about issues related to it with our heads.

@chetan_bhagat

Whatever the state of the economy, just happy that for a change the economy is the top issue on national news and not religion or caste.

288 replies/ 1,075 retweets/ 5,769 likes

The Three New I's of Indian Politics

Intention, initiative and ideas: Netas do not require anything more in a post-truth environment

Every Indian newspaper and magazine, and several notable publications worldwide, have carried their own take on demonetisation. Most of those analyses did a cost-benefit analysis of the move. Many intellectuals and leading economists have called the move questionable, simply on the basis of cold facts.

Most of the old cash has been declared and swapped in banks. This means that either (a) there wasn't that much black money in cash to begin with; and/or (b) the black money hoarders managed to swap the old black cash efficiently for new black cash.

Anecdotal reports suggest that the old cash was being swapped for new cash at rates as low as a mere 10 per cent commission. Bank officials around the country helped game the system (it really was like a video game, with the RBI adding new surprise rules on a daily basis).

While some deposited money could be declared in the latest version of the 'new' voluntary disclosure scheme, it is now widely accepted among intellectuals and economists that gains from the crackdown on black money were limited.

At the same time, many enumerate the costs of the demonetisation scheme as the following: a real slowdown in the economy that will reduce tax collections for the government and the earnings of many honest taxpayers; chances of a full blown recession along with loss of employment; millions of lost man hours that were spent in queues; and a loss of credibility for the Reserve Bank of India and the government as a whole because of the knee-jerk nature of the exercise as well as the ad hoc directives that they continue to churn out.

Well, they are not wrong. The true economic benefits of this exercise will be limited. Unless followed up by real measures to limit the generation of black money (including fixing thorough clean-up of political funding, a hotbed of black money generation), black money will continue to flourish in India.

However, none of this really matters in terms of the political impact the move has had on the BJP and Prime Minister Narendra Modi. For, politically, the move is a major hit. Sure, benefits are limited and the negative effects are many. However, interpreting demonetisation requires proper analysis, an understanding of the economy, and a rational perspective rather than an emotional approach.

All that already sounds tiresome and boring, doesn't it? The Indian voter has rarely cared about the economy while exercising his political preferences. What they loved about this move are the three I's that seem to result in big political gains for any leader who can display them: Intention, Initiative and Ideas.

Modi's intention was good. That alone fetches him high marks. In a country where the average politician is expected to be a corrupt goon who loots the nation, a leader who has the right intentions with regard to black money transactions is a huge plus.

No leader in his position had ever tried such a move. The fact that Modi showed initiative and that he didn't have to be pushed to do this, helps his case somewhat.

Finally, it was a relatively novel idea. Even though demonetisation has been tried before, nobody ever envisioned it or tried to execute it on this scale before.

Indians have long believed that there are 'lots' of rich people with 'lots' of black money which they keep under their mattresses, and that this is the root of India's problems. The exact amount of 'lots' is, of course, unknown. However, the demonetisation move resonated with that belief, and garnered near-unanimous support.

Never mind that the black money found in cash wasn't quite as much as people imagined. Or that in India there isn't a specific set of 'evil' people who are corrupt, but rather many ordinary people who become corrupt when given the chance (as when bankers swapped cash illegally).

What matters, emotionally speaking, to people is this: the PM tried something good, which he initiated on his own, and it was based on a fresh idea. That's enough for them to continue supporting him, and the move.

Something similar happened with the odd-even move to curb pollution in Delhi. Many experts argued that exhaust emissions from cars accounts for only a small fraction of the pollution in our cities, and that the exemptions would make the exercise futile. And they were right. Odd-even didn't help curb pollution. However, Chief Minister Arvind Kejriwal enjoyed public support because the move displayed the three I's.

Another example is Amma's canteens, and the entire gamut of freebie politics in Tamil Nadu. In practical terms, the scheme is unsustainable as the state would be burdened with massive debt due to such moves. However, people like it simply for the intention behind it.

Perhaps one day, cold facts and details of implementation and execution will matter more to the Indian people. For now, battered by a political class that never cared, just good intentions, a bit of initiative and fresh ideas seem enough.

YOUNG INDIA

'What out-of-control DU colleges can learn from uncool IITs' talks about why DU students as well as the administration must pull their socks up to fight political violence on campus and refocus on academic excellence.

'Indian Institutes of Politics' looks at the tragedy of Rohith Vemula's suicide and the role caste and politics played in this case. It also talks about an issue that confronts government universities—the level of autonomy the government gives to the university management—and this topic is also addressed in 'Indian Institute of Autonomy: Don't Kill a Model that Works'.

Finally, 'Letter to Kashmiri Youth' is an open letter to the Kashmiri youth, explaining why—if they care for their own futures, and for Kashmir—their best bet is to integrate their state to India.

What Out-of-control DU Colleges Can Learn from Uncool IITs

DU students as well as administration must pull their socks up to fight political violence on campus and refocus on academic excellence

Several decades ago, when we were students of IIT Delhi, my friends and I used to be insanely jealous of Delhi University colleges. Not only did they have a better female-to-male ratio than us, they were far more relaxed when it came to discipline.

The IITs kept us in the grind. We had over forty class tests, quizzes and mid-term tests every semester, all of which were factored into our grade point average. Class attendance was strictly monitored, and sometimes even contributed to our final score.

Meanwhile, our friends at DU couldn't party enough. They rarely attended classes. College for them meant addas on the campus lawns. Barring a handful of elite colleges (say, Stephen's or SRCC), academics was second priority.

Apart from rigour, IITs were also at a different level when it came to enforcing discipline. Any significant act of student indiscipline—skipping too many classes, breaking into a professor's office to steal a paper (yes, it has happened), vandalism, or inappropriate behaviour with women—met with one fate, the infamous DisCo or Disciplinary Committee. The DisCo never spares, used to be the adage. DisCo punishment could even mean expulsion from IIT, which meant a dark future.

Hence, IIT students had a reputation for being disciplined. We did have fun, including doing some barely legal stuff. However, we also paid attention to academics. And we never crossed a certain line even when it came to mischievous fun.

DU students, of course, showed no such restraint. They even had time for politics, and took campus elections seriously. Youth wings of national political parties dominated DU elections. There was something cool about those student leaders, bands around their foreheads, screaming about change. Joining busloads of students to roam from college to college, campaigning, seemed so much more fun than preparing for the next Applied Mechanics quiz.

IIT had student body elections too, but it was a low-key affair. Even posters weren't allowed on campus. Our politics was limited to cute horse-trading between hostels, a far cry from the highly charged atmosphere at DU.

We IITians weren't as cool as DU in some ways. However, we can safely say this—our students did really well in academics and got great jobs. And this is what they came to campus for. We also did not have the ugly violence that occurs in DU from time to time, as it did in Ramjas College in 2017.

We endlessly discuss the Ramjas incident, although we focus on the wrong issues when we do. We make it about tolerance vs intolerance, ABVP vs AISA, right vs left, BJP vs Congress, and ultimately, what every political debate in India gets reduced to these days—pro-Modi vs anti-Modi.

It's stupid. For the key issue is this: DU is out of control. The current management, including the vice-chancellor, the dean and the various college principals, simply cannot keep DU in check. This is a university that enrols the best students, yet seems to have little regard for academic rigour or discipline.

More than 95 per cent of the students who come to DU just want to study and build a good future. The failure to control the remaining 5 per cent, the goons, is harming the university's reputation, the atmosphere on campus and risking the future of all who study there. This can be fixed if there is a will to do so.

Why does DU have a system where it is okay to not attend classes and simply mug up for the exams at the end of the year? Why are the disciplinary committees so lax? How many students have been expelled from DU for engaging in violence in the past few years? Why do people who don't study in a particular college hang around in the college canteen? Is it a college or an adda? Why does all this happen at DU, but not at the IITs, IIMs, NDA or AIIMS?

There is nothing inherently wrong in students having political views or even an interest in politics. The line is crossed when they indulge in violent threats or actual violence. It is then that immediate, hard action must be taken so that nobody tries such a stunt again. Students must be kept busy through the duration of their course. And outsiders have no business hanging around the campuses.

It is about time the people who claim to be running DU actually took charge and prevented this great university from going out of control. As for the students, the best advice would be to focus on your studies and your future. It is good to have views on national issues. However, don't do it at the expense of deviating from your own life goals. Never allow yourself to be used by the media or politicians, and mess up your career in the process. Make the most of college life, by using it to make your future.

@chetan_bhagat

Tips to stay motivated: 1. Stay healthy. Exercise.
2. Have goals. make them focus of life 3. Only positive
people in your life. 4. Celebrate achievements of others.
Get inspired, not jealous 5. Spread smiles, not hate or
snarkiness on the Internet. 6. Love. Pray. Laugh.

152 replies/ 1,432 retweets/ 6,710 likes

Indian Institutes of Politics: Lack of Autonomy for Universities Is a Killer, Literally so in Rohith Vemula's Case

We must learn the right lessons from Rohith's suicide and change the way we run our universities

One of the saddest things that can happen in the world is when a young person takes his or her own life. It becomes particularly heartbreaking when the young person is educated, intelligent, sensitive and shows potential, yet feels he or she has no other option left.

This is what happened when Rohith Vemula, a twenty-five year old PhD scholar at the University of Hyderabad, took his own life after leaving a touching suicide note. Suicides can partly be linked to one's specific personality and mental makeup. However, some of it can—and in this case is—linked to the world around the person.

While Rohith's note blames no one for his death, he does mention his agony over being ostracised (he was suspended and asked to leave the hostel along with a few others), denied his due (his fellowship was delayed, causing financial hardship), and discriminated against.

A particular chain of events seems to have culminated in his suicide. Rohith was involved in student politics.

Apparently, he joined protests against Yakub Memon's hanging. During those protests, he had run-ins with ABVP students, who are backed by the BJP. An ABVP activist claimed that he was manhandled by Rohith and others, and a complaint was lodged. While such events are unsavoury, they are not unusual in Indian campuses, many of which are politically charged.

However, what happened next was unusual. The local MP, along with Union Labour Minister Bandaru Dattatreya, wrote a letter to HRD minister Smriti Irani, alleging that the university had become a 'den of casteist, extremist and anti-national politics'. The HRD ministry wrote to the university vice-chancellor, seeking to know what action was being taken.

Eventually, five students including Rohith were suspended and denied hostel accommodation. They camped outside the campus gates in a tent in protest. Rohith, unfortunately, committed suicide after a few days.

There is a clear conflict of interest when an ABVP complaint gets so much attention from two BJP-run Union ministries, which in turn can easily put pressure on the university to clamp down.

Meanwhile, politicians of all shades descended on the University of Hyderabad campus, particularly those that sought Dalit votes. I don't know what is sadder, a young man killing himself, or politicians flocking to the venue to increase their vote banks. This drama of blame-game politics on the issue will continue.

What we should focus on instead is deriving lessons from the incident. There are serious issues in the way we manage our universities, and it needs to be understood that Rohith's suicide is a horrible outcome of such mismanagement.

The single biggest issue confronting government universities is the level of autonomy the government gives to the university management. These institutions are run on taxpayer money, so clearly the government cannot take a completely hands-off approach. At the same time, should there be letters from Union ministries enquiring about specific cases involving students?

Should student discipline be a university issue, a local MP issue, a police issue or a Union ministry issue? Should government colleges even allow student politics on campus? Wouldn't campus politics create conflicts of interest and place students at risk, especially if they don't belong to the party that forms the government?

We don't know yet if the suspended students deserved punishment or not. However, who should be making this decision? If it is the university, should MPs be writing letters to ministers to take action, or equally bad, politicians from opposing sides descend on the university campus to decry the action? Why are we turning our universities into a joke? Isn't there enough silly politics around anyway?

Autonomy is the heart of the issue here, if not the only one. There are other aspects of the case that need to be discussed too. Why are government payments delayed so often? The university claims that Rohith's fellowship was delayed due to administrative issues and not out of vindictiveness. Even if one believes this, why are student stipends withheld for months at a time? Rohith's suicide note states that financial difficulties were a big factor in his taking his life.

Another issue is Rohith's presumed identity as a Dalit, and the discrimination Dalit students face on campus. It is a deplorable but unfortunate reality in a system where merit is given a backseat to identity. If we didn't have caste-based reservations, caste wouldn't be so relevant on campus. It would soon become a non-issue. If we can shift to an economic criteria for reservation rather than a caste-based one (today, we have the technology to do this), we can reduce the stigma associated with caste.

Unfortunately, caste reservations—the very scheme that was designed to make people more equal—has become the biggest cause of discrimination on every campus. It happened during my days at IIT, and it happens in every university with reservation today. Can't we switch to better admission criteria?

Politicians posturing and blaming each other on TV will achieve nothing. A genuine tribute to Rohith would be to learn the right lessons from his suicide. We need to make changes in the way we manage and run our universities. We also need to free our universities of caste and politics. Let's do it sooner rather than later, to prevent more cases like Rohith's in the future.

Indian Institute of Autonomy:
Don't Kill a Model that Works

To create and sustain world-class institutes of higher learning, maintain a balance between state control and institutional autonomy

I was once invited to join a panel discussion at a conference of vice-chancellors held at Rashtrapati Bhavan. To give credit where it is due, it was a well-organised and well-intentioned event. Nearly a hundred VCs of top central universities across India attended the conference.

The attendees, divided into several sub-groups, discussed the burning issues faced by the education sector today. Although the format of the meet was a tad too formal and colonial in protocol, the ideas were all current and relevant. The need to integrate industry-research-academia, using technology more effectively, driving innovation and entrepreneurship, tapping alumni bases, inter-university collaboration, and network connectivity—all these wonderful thoughts were discussed. Hence, the theory that the heads of our educational institutions are outdated and don't know what's going on in the world, was disproved.

And yet, few would disagree that there is plenty that needs to be done in the education sector.

If everyone in the country agrees on the wonderful ideas discussed in the conference, why doesn't it happen? Why isn't there more industry–university interaction, for instance? Why do we fall behind in cutting-edge research? Why don't we have more A-grade institutions? Why are the education brands created in the '60s and '70s—the IITs, IIMs, AIIMS, some Delhi University colleges and a couple of other places—the only reputed institutions in the country to date? Why haven't we created new brands in education, at par with IITs and the IIMs, in the '80s, the '90s or the new millennium?

The answer lies in our inability to manage an extraordinarily important issue affecting every state-owned institution in India—the question of autonomy. No matter how vocal and well-versed the academic heads were in that conference, the fact of the matter is that they won't be able to implement even 10 per cent of their ideas because their hands are tied. In India, the state funds the university and, hence, controls it. For our universities to thrive, the extent of control and the level of autonomy need to find an optimal balance.

For the IITs and the IIMs, the control–autonomy balance seems to have worked better than for the others. As a result, they could adapt better to changing times, attract top talent and maintain high standards of excellence over time. Small wonder, then, that their brand value exceeds that of the other institutes.

Of course, even IIMs are not immune to interference from the government. The new IIM bill of 2015, purportedly designed to make them statutory institutions so they can issue degrees instead of diplomas (a technicality for all practical purposes), is going to dramatically reduce the delicate autonomy balance that has helped the IIMs thrive.

To its credit, the government did place the draft bill for public consultation (on mygov.in). However, the proposed version is worded in a way that government approval will be required for almost all operations that matter—recruitment, enrolment, compensation and research. Needless to say, it will drastically reduce the autonomy of the IIMs and tilt the balance in favour of government control. IIMs, as we know them, will be changed forever.

Note the important distinction between full autonomy and balanced autonomy. A government-funded institution cannot be free of government control. Monitoring its performance or funding through annual reviews should be well within the government's purview. The problem occurs when it keeps the right to meddle at the operational level, interfering in the day-to-day running of the institution. Air India and ITDC hotels are visible examples of what happens when the government does that.

When you aspire to be world class, government interference on a daily basis can be devastating. It's important to understand that great educational institutions become great because of the people there— the faculty and the students. Otherwise, a college is just buildings and furniture. To be the best, you need a vital ingredient whose value is often ignored in India—top talent. Top talent, rare by definition, has the ability to innovate and execute, and thereby change a field. Top talent, which could come from anywhere, can transform a nation. The sad part is that we neither recognise it nor know how to manage it.

If you want world-class faculty to run an IIM, but have babus breathing down their necks, who in turn have netas looking over their shoulders, why would top talent want to join the institution in the first place? The salaries are already low (government job levels). Now, we also want them to obey whimsical orders from netas who care more about pleasing their constituencies than the world rankings of a top-class institute.

By definition, politics is inclusive. But excellence demands some exclusivity. If politicians run our finest educational institutions on a daily basis, constant clashes will be inevitable. That will only harm the institute. Why do it? Why mess up something good? Why not, in fact, liberate the other universities too? Release those VCs with great ideas and tied hands. Give them enough autonomy to create their own university brands. Monitor them, have checks and balances, but don't run the place.

The IIMs are not without flaws. They should be monitored and improved. However, killing the autonomy balance that has worked well for them so far would be counter-productive. Instead, we should replicate the model with other universities and generate more brands like the IIMs.

It would be a shame if we didn't know how to manage an institution that teaches, well, management.

@chetan_bhagat

Stone pelting is not kids playing with pebbles. It's a
violent attack with hard, heavy, rock-like stones thrown
at people. It is not an acceptable means of protest. Stop
glorifying it. Stop justifying it. Take action against those
doing it.

373 replies/ 2,866 retweets/ 9,028 likes

Letter to Kashmiri Youth: Even If You Don't Like India, Here's Why Your Best Bet Is to Integrate J&K With It

The youth of the Valley should take the lead in bringing it back into the Indian Union

Dear Kashmiri friends (the ones who don't like India),

I write in this open forum because something terrible is happening in the Kashmir Valley. The events at NIT Srinagar caught the entire nation's attention. Some students burst crackers when India lost the T20 semifinal. Many students were beaten for raising the Indian flag. Thereafter, bloody clashes broke out in north Kashmir.

I understand that there is little pro-India sentiment amongst locals in the Kashmir Valley. Many would rather the Valley be on its own, and some wouldn't even mind going over to Pakistan. I will not judge you. Despite being a patriotic Indian, I won't hold it against you if you hate India. You must and do have your reasons for it.

However, allow me to present another point of view. Allow me to tell you that your future will be brightest, on a practical basis, if the Kashmir Valley integrates with India. This is not an emotional, political or historical argument. It is simply more rational for people in the Kashmir Valley who seek a better future to do it in India.

Sure, the experts will jump on me now—experts who have made the Kashmir problem their fiefdom. Indeed, if the problem were solved, how would these people stay relevant? Hence, they will always attack any solution that is proposed for the Kashmir crisis with their elitist 'this is too complicated an issue' stance. They love 'complicated'. It gives them another conference to attend. You suffer with 'complicated', as the problem never gets solved.

The issue is complicated, for sure. For those who don't know the Kashmir issue, here it is in a nutshell. India became independent. The princely states were assimilated into the Indian Union. Jammu & Kashmir didn't accede. Pakistan attacked Kashmir, and took half of it (and still controls it). Kashmir's ruler called India for help. In return for this help, J&K became part of India, but with riders.

J&K would have its own constitution, and enjoy more political independence than other states, while the Centre would handle defence, foreign affairs and communications. In theory, it was a good solution, a sort of 'one country, two systems' approach. In reality, it never worked.

Instead of a child with two parents, as planned, J&K became nobody's child and an orphan. Pakistan took advantage of this situation and used the common factor of Islam to start a militant movement. The Indian Army tried to control it. However, it is difficult to control terrorism that co-exists with a civilian population (case in point: even the world's superpowers appear unable to control IS).

Thus, the Indian Army, and India, got a bad name in the Valley. Thus, the 'we hate India' slogans and the perennially unsolved Kashmir problem.

The question is, what is the Kashmiri youth to do now? First, it is important for everyone, not just Kashmiris, to understand the area and the people involved. The J&K map we see in Indian textbooks is nothing like what exists on the ground. Half of what we see on the map has been taken over by Pakistan and China. Even though India may still claim these territories, unless we are okay with heavy civilian casualties (which we are not), we will never recover them.

Hence, let's just focus on the half under Indian control, which can be divided into three areas: Ladakh, Jammu, and the Valley. Most of the trouble is in the Kashmir Valley. This is only around 7 per cent of the area that Indians see on the J&K map, approximately the size of Manipur. In terms of people, it is seven million, roughly the population of Chennai.

The terrain is rugged and the area is completely landlocked. Even if we were to indulge the argument that India is a terrible country and so Kashmir Valley should be on its own, can you really build a sustainable country out of this region? It will be a tiny stub of a state in a troubled area, abused by both India and Pakistan. With no real economy and extreme dependence on its giant neighbours, it risks becoming a cesspool of terrorism, drugs and smuggling.

There is also a risk of Kashmir being taken over by fundamentalist Islamic forces, if it separates. It is unlikely that any foreign investors would put their money in such a dangerous place. There would be no jobs and no safety. Would you want to live there? Ditto, if it joins Pakistan. India is seen as a major emerging market economy. Pakistan is not even seen as a real economy.

Another issue is women's rights. Half of the Valley's people are women. Given the hold of fundamentalist Islam, their rights would be curbed under both the independent Kashmir and Pakistan options. This half of the population would be better off with India. Or does what women want not matter?

If you are Kashmiri and care for Kashmir, the best option for you is to integrate with India. Your population is small, only around seven million. It is not impossible to unite them and create a group of people that talks real business with the Indian government. Your local politician won't talk assimilation, as he or she would rather hold more power than in a typical state government in India. However, for you, the youth, the best bet is to help make the Valley truly a part of India.

The rest of India should not ask for the removal of Article 370. The seven million people in the Valley should. The Kashmiri Pandits who were forced to leave the Valley need to be brought back. Terrorism is no solution, nor an adequate means of revenge and retribution for Indian atrocities. Terrorism harms people in the Valley, above all.

So, the need of the hour is for the youth in the Valley to start a movement to solve this problem. Get rid of Article 370. It does not empower Kashmir. It is only empowering your local politicians, who can do nothing for you without the cooperation of the Indian state.

Don't blame the Indian Army. It has the tough job of weeding out terrorists from a civilian population, which is almost impossible to do without collateral damage, terrible as that might be. However, blame those truly responsible—the Pakistani Army, the local leaders who exploited the situation, and the experts who did nothing for you.

Don't burst crackers when India loses. Don't feel good when India fails. Because, if India fails, you will fail too.

Jai Hind. Jai Kashmir.

Concluding Thoughts:
Staying India Positive

I have written about Indian economy, society, politics and youth issues for over ten years now. This decade is also the period over which we have experimented with various kinds of governments and leaders. Over these ten years, while my writing on issues that concern the nation continues, I am also gradually shifting focus to the subject of the self-development of the individual. The more I think about it, the more I am convinced that the two go hand in hand. The system must be improved slowly, but the self-improvement of citizens is an essential step in progressing as a country.

Suggesting how we can help our country develop and keep our governments accountable will continue to be important. Democracy, when left unchecked, can go haywire. We as citizens have to stay alert to that.

But while we patiently wait for the big changes, India's youth also need to focus within and continue to develop themselves to counter the shortcomings of the system.

As you finish reading this book, I urge you to keep this India Positive mindset—where we strive to find solutions to the country's problems rather than criticising its failures in a negative spirit, and believe in personal growth as well as national progress. All the best for the future! And stay (India) positive!